My Grandma Surfs
Better Than You

Mike + Holly,
Surf for life !!!!
Live Aloha

♡

My Grandma Surfs Better Than You

A Women's Guide to Catching More Waves

By Kim Hamrock

Kim Hamrock

Registration #: VAUU998048

Date: September 24, 2009

Effective Registration Date: April 4, 2008

ISBN-13:978-1541222106
ISBN-10:1541222105

THIS BOOK IS DEDICATED
TO MY GRANDCHILDREN

OLIVER AND TALLULAH
My favorite surf groms

All my respect to

KING NEPTUNE AND MOTHER OCEAN

I'm grateful for all the good waves that I've ever surfed,
and every wipeout that I've survived.

FROTHY WAVES CURLING
CRESTING HIGH FROM DISTANT SHORES
SURFING DOLPHINS PLAY

- ANOYNOMOUS OLD SURFER

ACKNOWLEDGMENTS

First and foremost, I want to acknowledge my kids for all their love and tolerating all the years I competed and dragged them to the beach. Thank you to all of you who have donated and helped with this project. Special thanks, to my Aunt Susan. Marlon Bunch for his loving and moral support. Dr. Kathleen Campbell, D.C., for keeping my spine aligned (especially after getting worked at Pipeline). To my sponsors, for all their support throughout the years. The pioneer women surfers, who helped paved the way. My brothers and neighborhood boys, for making me tough. The boys at Upper Trestles, for naming me "Danger Woman". To anyone and everyone who has ever shared a wave with me (or not burned me). To the surf judges, who have scored me fairly. To my surf buddy Sophia Tiare Bartlow (1990 - 2017) - Surf in Peace. To my Dad for showing me how to paddle. Most importantly, to my Mom for teaching me that I could be whatever I wanted when I grew up.

Contributing Editors: Lee Evans, Dr. Bruce 'Snake' Gabrielson, Ph.D., Mike Davis, Jamie Heraver.

Artist/Cartoonist: Kim Hamrock
Graphic Artist: Matt Bruns

Contents

Kim Hamrock and the original Danger Woman (Mom)

Kim at Puerto Escondido

Kim Hamrock – Inductee Surfing Walk of Fame 2005

INTRODUCTION

"Why does everyone call you Danger Woman?"

Do you know how many times I have been asked that question? In the beginning, I would simply shrug my shoulders and say, "I don't know?" Then I started making up a variety of answers. On many occasions, I simply took the fifth. Truly, it was the boys down at Trestles who gave me this nickname. Therefore, if you really want to know, you'd have to ask one of them. Keep in mind, this is only my perspective on why I believe they called me *Danger Woman.*

Have you ever wondered what is really going on among the surfers out in the waves? What is the proper protocol? Who has priority for the wave? How do you prevent from being run over by another surfer? *"My Grandma Surfs Better Than You"* will give you the insight into these questions and much more. This is an instructional book with an unorthodox view on surfing etiquette, and further, how to catch more waves. You'll learn where and where not to surf, and how to work your way into any surf lineup.

Additionally, it's a book about doing whatever it takes to get waves within the limits of the unwritten rules of surfing. Now keep in mind, I've been known to break all of the rules. Eventually, I learned how to conform to them. Then, I started experimenting with wave catching strategies. Included is my philosophy about surfing and the sociological aspects of what it was like to be a woman learning to surf in the seventies. Packed with *true-life* stories, here is some of the wisdom I've learned along the way.

Fighting for waves, the constant hassles and ongoing teasing from the boys, was very frustrating. In retrospect, I can now see it was the training grounds for personal growth. This provided me with an opportunity to turn negative experiences into positive ones. Best of all, these confrontations helped me become a better surfer. What's more, they made me tough mentally and physically! This really was helpful when surfing in big dangerous waves! Believe me, you need nerves of steel and have to know how to take a beating.

There is no aspect of surfing that isn't comparable to other experiences I've had in everyday life. This knowledge has helped me through some very difficult times, both in and out of the surf. Needless to say, starting my surfing career at an older age was challenging. The exception, however, was the self-confidence that came with maturity. I watched many young girls (and boys) become discouraged with surfing politics and quit competing. It's not in my nature to give up. Truth be told, I would've quit too if I wasn't so determined (some call it stubborn), to obtain a world title. I believe if you have a strong enough desire and don't waiver from your goals, you will succeed. You just have to decide how bad you want something and what you are willing to sacrifice to get it.

During my formative years of surfing, I would recall my Dad's advice, *"Two wrongs don't make a right, but it sure does make you feel better."* Well, I really took those words to heart. Whatever the boys did to me out in the surf, I would do back to them. If they did it again, I would do it back twice. This went on for years – Wave after wave, day after day. Finally, I realized this wasn't such good advice after all.

Here are some better words of wisdom that my Dad taught, *"Behavior tells all."* Observing people's actions will tell you more about them than their words. This is why I feel it's more powerful to teach through example, forgiving others, sharing, and being a positive influence. Yet, I had to do more than know these new and improved methods. I had to *live* them before I could pass them on to others.

That said, I reveal my tricks of the trade, which I discovered as a woman surfer. The following stories will give you insight into my wave-catching strategies. Overcoming these obstacles enabled me to become a world-class surfer. Also, it helped me develop my unique surfing style. I am known in the industry for taking risks and fearlessly assaulting the big surf. Perhaps this is one of the reasons why the boys nicknamed me *Danger Woman?*

Along with surfing etiquette, included are sections regarding safety and localism. There's a glossary for those unfamiliar with surf lingo. Most importantly, these written (and some previously unwritten), rules are for the safety of both the novice and expert surfers.

The intent of this book is to primarily educate you concerning the nuances of surfing etiquette. Additionally, it will give you some insight on the challenges (and rewards), of being a woman surfer. Of course, I trust it'll help you catch more waves too!

NOTE TO THE NOVICE SURFER AND THOSE WHO DON'T SURF

I suggest reading the Glossary, along with Chapters 17 and 18 first. This will help familiarize you with the surf terminology and the basic surfing rules and etiquette.

Enjoy the stories, learn from them and have a good laugh!

Kim *'Danger Woman'* Hamrock

1 - DANGER GIRL

How many kids truly know what they want to do when they grow up? This was never a problem for me. The moment I became aware that surfing existed I knew that's what I wanted to do. The fact that I was a little kid and lived 20 miles inland didn't deter me whatsoever. Of course, I had no idea how, or when I'd surf, I simply knew I would. Before we begin let me share a bit of my pre-surfing history with you.

It all started when I was about four years old. This is when I would sit (or stand) on my Mom's redwood rolling plant caddie, and ride it down the walkway that went from our kitchen to the garage. There was a slight downhill slope that was bordered by the lawn (this gave me a soft landing for the wipe outs). The problem was that the caddie kept spinning out of control when I tried to make it go straight. For this reason, I decided to rip the wheels off and take the plant caddie apart. Next, I hammered the wheels onto one of the single planks of wood that was from the caddie. Voila! Now I had a functional riding toy. Inadvertently, I had made my own skateboard before knowing they even existed. However, I got in a lot of trouble for destroying my Mom's planter. At least I got to keep my new toy! In any event, I rode it every day all day long, well at least after all my chores were done. Because my parents noticed how much enjoyment I got from riding my toy, they bought me roller-skates for Christmas. Yet, I didn't like that they were strapped to my shoes and I couldn't jump off when I got going too fast.

Predictably, before the day was over I took the wheels off of my brand new skates and searched the yard for a flat, narrow piece of wood. Once I found the ideal piece, I grabbed a hammer and some nails and attached the roller skate wheels onto the board. Since the wheels from the skates were clay, not metal like the ones from the plant caddy, I now had improved my version of a skateboard. At least now I could jump off when I needed to! Although I was proud of myself for my new design, my parents were upset and I got in trouble again, this time for ruining the brand-new skates. As far as I was concerned, my modifications made the skates better. Little did I know that I was practicing for a lifetime of surfing.

A few years later (being six or seven years old now) I was watching television when *The Wide World of Sports* came on featuring surfing championships. Absolutely fascinated, I watched the program in awe trying not to blink, afraid that I might miss something. Surfing was the coolest thing I'd ever seen! In fact, this is when I knew my calling in life, to surf. This was confirmed when I saw women surfing too! In retrospect, I believe one of them was Linda Benson. In her day Linda surfed better than most of the guys! Also, she was the first woman surfer (besides the ancient Hawaiian Queens) to fearlessly charge the big waves at Waimea Bay, Hawaii. Although she's in her seventies now she is still a fantastic surfer.

In any case, when the first commercial break came on I ran into the kitchen to tell my Mom that I was going to surf. When I shared my exciting news, her friend (who was visiting) told me that she surfed all the time. This was a profound moment for me! Her friend was now my new hero simply because she surfed. Wow! I couldn't believe I already knew a real surfer!

The first woman I saw surfing (not on T.V.), was Jericho Poppler Bartlow (of course, that was years later). Notably, I was very fortunate because she was one of the top pro women surfers at the time. What a treat! Not only that, but her beautiful surfing style, and how she charged the waves so gracefully, was very impressive. Because Linda and Jericho were the first women I saw surfing, it's no wonder I developed a more progressive style. This is how I thought all women surfed!

Needless to say, it was a long time before I saw any other women surfing, except for a few quick clips of them surfing here and there in a surf flick (mostly they just showed girls on the beach in skimpy bikinis). Also, it was rare to see any photos of women surfers in the surf mags. At this stage of the game, I was still a kook and couldn't even turn my board. Yet, I aspired to become a great surfer like these women. Overall there weren't that many women surfers to emulate. The exception was the charging power surfers like Joyce Hoffman, Lynn Boyer, Brenda Scott, and of course Margo Godfrey Oberg. Actually, quite a few of the first pro women surfers ripped. I truly admired Rell Sunn because not only did she surf beautifully, but she also represented the ultimate overall water woman. Yet, my primary role models were the men. I wanted to surf like them.

Fortunately, my Mom took my brothers and me to the beach frequently. For the most part, we went every day during the summers. Because we didn't have surfboards, we body surfed, rode on rubber mats or played in the surf on inner tubes. We skim boarded too. When we were at the beach I'd spend the entire day in the ocean and never wanted to get out of the water (I'm still like that). Since my Mom didn't know how to swim she'd have to repeatedly yell at me to come in for lunch. After pretending I didn't hear her for as long as I thought I could get away with, reluctantly I'd finally come in. Also, she'd make me wait that stupid half hour after you eat so you wouldn't get a cramp. I hated that wait! Hence, it wasn't uncommon for me to bug her every few minutes to go back into the water until she was so annoyed she'd just let me go.

On another note, our Grandpa owned a cabin in the local mountains, at Lake Gregory, where we used to rent paddleboards. Our Dad would put us on the paddleboards when we were still babies before we could even walk. By the same token, he'd paddled us around until we got big enough to paddle on our own. In other words, I've pretty much been paddling my entire life. Although I'd spent so much time at the beach, I'd still never seen anyone surfing like I had on television. This was hard to believe since we went to all the local beaches like Huntington, Newport, and Laguna. I was even at the jetty in Corona Del Mar during the famous big swell in 1969, but that's another story.

Kim Learning to Paddle with her brothers - Lake Gregory, CA

Anyway, when I was older I acquired a 'real' skateboard. Skateboarding was a big fad in the 60's and 70's. It used to be called 'sidewalk surfing'. This is when I started skateboarding with my older brothers and neighbor boys, with whom I was always trying to keep up with. They would encourage me to go faster, turn harder, and not be a sissy. My middle brother and I customized a water ski by attaching skateboard wheels to it. We bombed down the hills in our neighborhood riding tandem on it. This would scare me and I would beg him to slow down. He'd just laugh and go faster. Unfortunately, I was always in the front. This sucked because when we fell he would grab me so he could land on me instead of the pavement.

We also rigged up our six-foot long toboggan to skate on, but mostly we rode it sitting down. We would bribe our little brother into joining us. With three of us on the toboggan, we went super fast. My oldest brother had a friend who would drive us, with our toboggan, to the biggest steepest hills around. One advantage, besides not having to lug the toboggan uphill, was with his van following us we didn't have to worry about cars coming up from behind us. His friend used the speedometer to time how fast we could go. Our record speed was a little over forty miles per hour. Oh, my God, did we have some hideous wipeouts! We rode our toboggan skateboard repeatedly until the time we almost ended up under a car. If our Mom only knew the half of what we did!

After that last near-death experience, I decided to ride solo. I continued to get more experienced, and more daring, bombing down all the big hills in the Heights where I lived. My goal was to try to get at least ten runs in every day after school before it got dark. On weekends I'd skate from dawn to dusk, except when I was riding my mini-bike. I was as addicted to skateboarding then as I am to surfing now! What was really cool was if you hiked up our private drive to the top of the hill, you could skate back down around the hill to the bottom of our driveway. This was a mile long run! From there, you could continue down through the valley for another mile if you wanted. I would stop after the steepest part unless I was going to meet my friends at the mall.

By the way, the first mile is like riding a wave at San Onofre, slow and mushy. The next quarter mile is like surfing Sunset Beach, Hawaii. This is because you had to continuously turn to keep from going too fast and losing control. Usually, I'd just take-off down our private drive and skate the gnarlier part of the hill. Also, I enjoyed skating at night whenever the moon was full. Actually, it was safer because you could see the lights of the cars before they got too close. Believe it or not, whenever I get the chance I still bomb these hills at fifty some years old!

Sometimes the city boys would challenge me to a downhill race. By all means, I wasn't the fastest, but I was the most familiar with the road and fast enough. There was no doubt I had it dialed-in and knew exactly when to slow down to avoid getting the speed wobbles. Even though I'd yell out a warning for them to slow down, they never listened. The guys out front always fell on the last (and steepest) part of the run, getting a bad case of road rash. Trust me, I've left plenty of layers of my own flesh on that road! No doubt I felt bad for them, yet I'd still laugh as I flew past them across the finish line. I was undefeated. Whenever I was skateboarding I'd pretend that I was surfing. Even though my surfing days were still yet to come, between skateboarding, paddle-boarding, and all the time I spent playing in the ocean, the foundation had been laid.

Finally, in 1973 (I was almost thirteen years old), I got the opportunity to surf. This was in Hawaii. My total spending money for the trip was $11.00, which happened to be the exact amount to rent a surfboard. After renting the board, my youngest brother and I dragged it across the beach, paddled out and caught our very first waves together, surfing tandem. We were used to paddling together because of our experience on the paddleboards at the lake. This made it easy for us to catch the slow rolling waves off Waikiki Beach. After my short surfing experience in Hawaii (barely an hour) I was more surf-crazed than ever! Yet it was still almost another year before I got the opportunity to surf again.

The second time I surfed was down in Mexico (no wonder Hawaii and Mexico are my favorite places to surf). From the time I was eight years old, my next-door neighbors would take my brothers and me to their trailer in Cantamar (Baja California). I always wanted to surf there but none of us had surfboards. Mostly we rode mini bikes down the beach to the nearby sand dunes. That's what this area was famous for. Finally, when we got a little older my middle brother and his friend Mike brought surfboards with them. My brother wouldn't let me use his board so one afternoon while he and his friend were off collecting bottles I decided to "borrow" it. They would trade the bottles in for money to buy beers. (A habit I too had since I was younger than I want to mention!) Therefore, I took his board out hoping he'd be gone for a while, sneaking off to drink his beers. As I still do, I lost track of time while surfing because of having so much fun. Therefore, I didn't come in before he returned. When I did come in I ended up getting yelled at and beaten up. This wouldn't be the last time I stole his board and went surfing. In fact, I did it every opportunity I got until the day came when I finally got my own surfboard (it was worth the beating every time). My first board was a 5'8" David Nuuiwha *Dyno Fish* (twin fin). From the start I had no problem catching waves and standing up. It was when I tried to turn that I kept falling.

Due to being an inlander without a car, it wasn't until I was about sixteen that I was able to start surfing consistently. Unfortunately, for the first several years I was what you'd call a weekend warrior. Yet, from then on there was no stopping me. This was the beginning of surfing for the rest of my life. At this stage, besides learning how to turn, I still had a lot to learn about surf etiquette and how to get along with others in the water.

When I first started surfing I had no clue what it would take to catch waves in a crowd, but it didn't take long to find out. The first thing I had to do was get over feeling intimidated when I was competing with the boys to catch a wave.

2 - THE TEN YEAR OLD WITH TOO MUCH TESTOSTERONE

Characteristically, in most societies, females are hesitant to behave aggressively. This was especially true in the sixties when I was raised. My Mom taught me to be well mannered, and conduct myself with proper *ladylike* behavior: Keep my legs crossed. Speak only when spoken to. Don't call the boys – Let them call you, that type of mentality.

In a territorial surfing environment, being a nonassertive female didn't get you many waves. Unless of course, you happened to be really cute, could barely surf, or were wearing a sexy little bikini. In other words, as long as you weren't a threat to taking one of the 'boys' waves they most likely wouldn't hassle you. In the surfing world (and especially by my competitors), I am known to be a charger with an aggressive style of surfing. What they don't know is why. Of course, part of it's just who I am and the rest was a learned behavior. It took courage to overcome my apprehension of being aggressive as a female surfer. Yet, it only took one incident that really accelerated the process.

When I was still in the beginning stages of learning how to surf, I got hassled by a little kid. This incident took place at T-Street, in San Clemente. There was a clean two to three-foot swell breaking, making the waves ideal for a beginner. However, every time I tried to catch a wave, this little gnat of a ten-year-old boy, with an overabundance of testosterone, kept snaking me. He'd paddle over, under or around me snatching up all the waves. He was super aggro and appeared to be on a mission to make sure that I didn't get any waves. After doing this to me several times, I had enough. Disregarding everything my Mother taught me about proper *ladylike* behavior, I thought: *Screw manners! This just isn't working for me.*

Besides, I figured the only way to catch a wave would be to surf as aggressive as he was. Certainly, it was working for him, so why not me? For that reason, I tried it out. From then on, whenever there was a wave I wanted, I'd paddle as hard as I could to out-position him (or anyone for that matter). The first wave I finagled from him started his yapping.

When I paddled back out into the lineup, he got in my face and started yelling at me. "Hey! You're a girl! You shouldn't be so aggro!"

I responded very politely, "When I was being mellow you kept taking all the waves from me. Why don't you be more of a gentleman and share? Really, aren't you supposed to let ladies go first?" Of course, this did not sit well with him. With that being said, I rapidly spun my board around to catch another wave. Sinking my arms deep into the water I took a few quick strokes and was surfing down the line before he knew what happened. When I paddled back out he was still sitting there contemplating how I managed to snag another wave from him.

Before he had time to say anything, I grabbed *another* wave he thought he was entitled to. Dumbfounded, I'm sure he was wondering how everything had changed so quickly.

After that, I paddled away and tried to keep my distance. Then he started paddling towards me yelling, "Hey!" When there was no response, he yelled again to get my attention. "Hey!"

However, hoping this little twerp of a boy would go away, I continued ignoring him. "*Hey!*" he shouted louder in his annoying little prepubescent voice, "Girls don't belong in the water anyway!" It was at that moment I decided not to let anyone push me around anymore! This was the starting point of paddling my hardest for waves, and learning how to get comfortable surfing aggressive around guys. Since then, many guys have attempted to intimidate me into not going for a wave, or luring me into dangerous ones. It didn't work! All this did was make me become more determined to catch the waves I wanted.

In retrospect, I could thank that bratty little kid (and you guys can curse him) because from that day forward, I became a more assertive surfer. Also, I started catching a helluva lot more waves! By closely observing the guys, they'd inadvertently taught me all the dirty tricks to catching more waves. This is what prompted me to come up with some of my own wave catching techniques! For the most part, it was just another day in the life of a woman surfer, surfing back in the seventies.

3 - LIFE OF A WOMAN SURFER

The surfing scene back in the seventies was certainly different from how it is now. It wasn't uncommon to see fist fights in the water on a regular basis. Guys punched each other out, had yelling matches and even kicked their boards out at anyone who dropped in on them. For the most part, the guys were too intimidating for most women to even consider surfing. Of course, I had waited so long to start surfing that nothing was going to deter me. Because the first few years I surfed was primarily at Trestles, The Ranch or on the Central Coast, I rarely saw other girls surfing.

These days there are lots of women from all walks of life around the world who surf. Consequently, there are some days when there are more girls in the lineup than there are boys! In addition, now women surfers have their own clothes, magazines, books, wetsuits, shops, surf schools, clubs, contest, etc. They even make cute little bathing suits that actually stay on while surfing. Wow, imagine that! Function *and* fashion!

Growing up with three brothers and a neighborhood full of mostly older boys, I'd been prepared for any type of attitude in the surf. This was a good thing too because my boyfriend warned me that if I got into any trouble – I was on my own. This is why I had to learn how to take care of myself. Part of the *Danger Woman* reputation came from not backing down from the guys and charging the waves no matter how big they were.

Through trial and error, mostly error, I gradually learned the rules of surfing. Fortunately, surfing came naturally for me. Although I could paddle and catch waves from the start, it still took a while to improve my skills. Learning how to surf was even more challenging because the boys didn't want me out there to begin with. It seemed I was constantly hassled and ended up getting yelled and cursed at. There were plenty of boards shot out at me too. Also (like most novice surfers), I got a few bonks on the head from my own surfboard and others in the process.

At the time it never occurred to me that you could take surf lessons. Really, surf schools were unheard of (except for the Hawaiian Beach Boys). In reality, it was quite the contrary. In those days the guys would rather hassle another surfer (boy or girl), to prevent them from learning, than help them out. Besides, discouraging a new surfer enough to make them want to quit was just another tactic used to control the rapidly growing crowds. For this reason, it wasn't easy trying to catch a wave (especially with no one else on it). Unfortunately, when I would finally catch a good wave, the boys would drop in on me. In retaliation, I started *hopping* them back (or was it the other way around)? Regardless, this began a ten-year war and the name-calling that came with it. The boys had a variety of nicknames for me. *Animal Woman, Jungle Woman, Witchy Woman* (this one they sang to me) and who knows what else! Eventually, they gave me the name that stuck, *Danger Woman*.

Of course, my friends and I had plenty of names for these guys too: *The Blue Baboon* (due to his stance and the bright blue color of his wetsuit) and 6'4" (the tall dude). There was *Twidgo-Twadgo* (who still gets up on one knee before standing up), *The Walrus* (the self-proclaimed *Mayor of Trestles*), *Pete and his Love Monkey*, (you don't want to know why)! Also, there was *Knockwurst* and *Bratwurst, along with Danger Duck*, just to name a few.

Little did I know what the life of a woman surfer would be. Growing up in a "man's world" I'd always been comfortable hanging out with the guys. However, in the male dominant sport of surfing, being a female surfer was challenging. Most of the time I didn't even think about being a girl, I'd just go out and do what I loved to do the most – Surf. The guys who brought it to my attention were usually the mean ones. These were the dudes who felt threatened with a woman surfing in *their* ocean, participating in *their* sport, catching *their* waves. Although most of the guys were way cool, there were still lots of bullies. Thank God there are men who enjoy the women out surfing with them. Also, there are those who at least *pretend* not to mind. But then again, there are the ones who make it very obvious that surfing is no place for a woman, period! Surfing for over forty years and dealing with all kinds of confrontations, I still believe the cool dude's way outnumber the rude ones. Yet, for some reason, I seem to have a knack for attracting the obnoxious ones.

Surprisingly enough, being a traveling female surfer ended up being fairly advantageous. Maybe it's easier for a girl to strike up a conversation with a guy regarding the surf conditions. They probably didn't take girls seriously. The first thing I'd ask them was where the best place to paddle out was. Next, I wanted to know when the best tides for surfing were. What's the lineup? Are there any dangers to be aware of (like rocks, rips, reefs, sea life)? Are the locals friendly? The guys were generous with the information they shared. Although, they may have regretted it later when they saw how many waves I caught due to their help.

Once I first started surfing halfway decent, I got into a gnarly fight. I was barreling down a wave at Trestles when some kook went left (Upper Trestles is a right-hand point with only an occasional left during a south swell. This was not the case at the time). Well, this guy slammed straight into me, which caused me to go flipping through the air. In the process, I heard the crack of two boards colliding, which left a big ding on my brand new board. Primarily, I was mostly pissed because he ruined my ride. It took so much effort to get a good wave there by myself. With these thoughts in mind, I started yelling at him for dinging my board. Before I knew it he swung a punch at me just barely clipping me in the jaw. Good thing I saw it coming and went underwater to help soften the blow. At that point, full of adrenaline, I went all *Three Stooges* on him. Hence, I poked him in the eyes with two fingers of one hand holding him under water this way. This left the other hand free in case I had to slug him back. A couple of times I started to let him up, but then decided to wait until he was closer to drowning. This was to be certain he'd be too breathless to retaliate and fight back when I did let him up!

My next-door neighbor Craig, one of the boys who had encouraged me to surf since I was a Grom, was nearby and quickly came to the rescue. Being a knee-boarder, his swim fins enabled him to stay up high in the water. He grabbed the kid (we were both kids), by the hair with one hand and started pounding on him with the other. Assisting him, I grabbed the guy by the hair and held him up so Craig could use both fists (I had witnessed him practicing punches like this on his speed-bag many times). My boyfriend saw what was happening and paddled over. This is when Craig quit punching him and I let go. Still gasping for air, the kid started protesting that he didn't know I was a girl. Come on? My hair was braided, I was wearing earrings, and I was on a pink surfboard (P.T. was the only guy who rode pink surfboards then). My boyfriend grabbed the kid's board and shoved it across the water knocking him in the mouth, drawing blood. Like I said earlier my boyfriend always warned me that I was on my own, so I was surprised (and grateful) when he came over to help.

Next thing you know, the guy's friends started paddling over yelling loudly and acting all tough ready to fight. No doubt, they're thinking it was going to be an easy fight with five of them against three of us, one of us being a girl. What they didn't realize was that there were really eight of us. My other surf buddies saw what was happening and paddled over to the commotion. Before anything more happened they told the kid and his friends to get out of the water and split. Because my friends were super built and fit, there wasn't much of an argument. There were a few half-assed grumbles as the kid and his friends paddled in but that was about it. They were also warned that they'd better never be caught surfing there again. Although the guys did leave, stupidly enough they showed up the following week. This time they did get their asses kicked and were sent home for the second time. We never saw them surfing there again. Welcome to the good old days!

These friends who helped me out had been surfing Trestles on a regular basis for years. They were the same guys I grew up skateboarding with. The ones who always wanted me to go surfing with them, telling me how good I'd be. That was when I was only ten and they were sixteen, so there was no way in Hell my Mom would let me go surfing with them. Nevertheless, I continued to beg her to let me go surfing.

Getting back to the story, unfortunately, this incident took place the very first time my Mom came to watch me surf. She saw the fight going on out in the water. To her horror, she realized that her daughter was right in the middle of it! When I came in, I told her not to worry there were always fights in the water. That was the first, and one of the very few times that I'd ever been in a physical fight while surfing. Besides the tussle with Jimmy Hogan, which apparently was a case of mistaken identity (he thought I was someone else). Many years later I came to find out that it was rumored I was a black belt! Looking back it's possible these brawls may have had something to do with that rumor. Maybe that's why I never got beat up?

During this era of surfing, there was also the *'anti-contest'* mentality. In other words, you were either a soul surfer or a competitive surfer.

There was no compromise. The guys I grew up surfing with were clearly part of the *'anti-contest'* group. Thus, this perspective is the reason I didn't start competing until I was a month shy of my thirtieth birthday (and a mother with three kids). Being naturally competitive, I secretly wanted to compete.

The other mindset in those days was your ability as a surfer was determined by how well you surfed the big waves in the islands. To be specific, the North Shore of Oahu, Hawaii. This factor had a huge affect on why I've always charged the biggest waves I could. Really, I didn't know any better. Plain and simple, I thought this was the only way you could be a *real surfer*. Eventually, I wanted to prove that you could be both, a soul surfer *and* a competitor.

Admittedly, when I first started competing I was totally clueless. Believe it or not, I'd never even been to a surf contest! This is why I was completely oblivious about surf competitions and the politics involved. After only a few contests, it was apparent something wasn't right. To the best of my knowledge, I was adhering to the *'judging criteria' ?*

Too many times it appeared that the contest directors weren't following their own rules. Inadvertently, I had thrown a wrench into their plans of grooming the next batch of young California pro women surfers. As a result, I felt as though I had to surf twice as good as the other women for half the points. Yet, this is what made me even more determined to surf better and keep doing my best to win!

Throughout my competition era, I spent most weekends (and some holidays) competing. The majority of traveling was done up and down the California coast where the family would accompany me. Yet, there was the occasional out of state or overseas traveling. This was usually when I was on the U.S.A. Surf Team, or competing for a national title. I had a goal to win the U.S. Championships on all four coasts (California, Florida, Texas and Hawaii) before going pro. On these trips, I had to go solo. When the kids couldn't go with me they would stay mostly with their Grammy, or at home with their dad.

At first, the whole family enjoyed going, but as the kids got older they had other interests. After a while, they were tired of going to so many "stupid" surf contests. At that point, they could decide if they wanted to go or not. Sometimes only one of the kids would join me for a special one-on-one trip. Then, it was mostly my youngest daughter and her friends that went with me on these mini surf safaris. Between balancing my family life, competing, sponsors, and managing my own surf school, it's a wonder I acquired any titles! It took a tremendous amount of focus.

There were many different reasons why I competed. One of them was because for years the guys kept telling me how much better I surfed than the other girls. They were constantly asking me why I didn't compete. This made me curious to see how I'd fare in the competition arena. Of course, I wanted to compete just to travel and surf a variety of different breaks too. We always went to the same beaches so this was a way to explore new surf spots and expand my wave knowledge. There were some personal reasons why I competed too that I wasn't even aware of until years later.

After experiencing a few contests, it was apparent the girls needed to improve their surfing skills. Unbeknownst to my competitors, it became part of my mission to help raise the level of women's surfing. Believe me, I wasn't going to make it easy for them either! Tough love. If the girls could take-off deeper, or out paddle me, well then they could have the wave. Truthfully, I pushed them hard. This was the main reason I competed for so long, besides wanting to acquire a world title.

Currently, the girls are surfing incredibly well and shredding up the waves! On top of that, they are starting to surf younger and younger! These little girl groms surf fearlessly. On the whole, the Aussie and Brazilian girls surf the most aggressive and are powerful surfers. There have been some outstanding women surfers from the U.S. Mainland (Kim Mearig, Frieda Zamba, Lisa Anderson to name a few), but overall the American women's surfing at the time was still weak. The Hawaiian girls are beautiful surfers. They have it all, style, power and grace. I'm happy to say that women's surfing throughout the world has progressed immensely making all my efforts worth it. In fact, it's just been announced that they have added women's big wave surfing to the tour! Keep going girls! Take it to the next level! I'm so proud of all of you. Remember, "You don't need balls to charge!"

The only time I shared waves during a competition was with the Hawaiian women. In return, they took me to their hidden reef breaks and shared their beautiful Hawaiian culture. Other than that I was ruthless. Seriously, I enjoyed challenging the girls (and guys) to surf harder. This was done by pushing the limits and going for it. Big or small. Do or die, win or lose. Trust me, I was a fierce competitor. Certainly, this inspired many but pissed off most. Feeling loved and hated with an equal passion was conflicting, but at least it was passion! Obviously, conforming is not one of my stronger points. I never did fit in – Girls were jealous, guys were threatened. Me, I merely wanted to surf. Oh and another thing, I never tired of winning, which I wanted to accomplish through my surfing. Therefore, keeping my dignity, I never lost my temper. Instead, I would simply smile and keep showing up. Nor did I kiss-up to the judges, date the photographers, or hang onto the coat tails of the top pro surfers for a free ticket around the world. My motto was: "*I don't kiss ass – I kick ass!*"

In pursuit of a world surfing title, I ended up developing a bit of a chip on my shoulder and started expecting to be burned in contests. When the director finally decided to crown me a world champion, it was in hopes that I'd retire. No joke, he asked me the next day when I was on my way to celebrate by having a local beverage and smoke a big Cuban cigar! That was my tradition whenever I won a major competition. I'd go off and sit by myself and think, "Fuck yeah!"

Now don't get me wrong, competing wasn't all bad. There were so many wild fun times we had in the process! For instance, well I better not say! It was all pretty classic traveling up and down the coast surfing along the way. There were times when we would sneak a dozen people at a time into one hotel room. Complimentary breakfasts were totally devoured. Most often we'd take turns staying at each other's houses (it depended on who lived closest to the contest site). We'd all party together the night before then compete the following morning. The best part was all the beautiful lifelong friends I've made along the way. So many characters! I am still, and will forever be, a soul surfer! I love my surfing buddies.

Regardless, whether I was competing or free surfing, it seemed I was always being challenged. This eventually turned me into a surf animal. Frustrated, my justification for misbehaving in the lineup was for all the torment that I'd been through.

Unknowingly, I ended up repeating the same behavior I detested. I didn't even realize how gnarly I'd become. Attitude is so important. This seems simple now, but it took me quite a while to figure it out. Who knows? What I do know is I felt as though I had to earn every wave I caught. Yet, through it all, I still didn't lose my deep love of surfing simply for the sake of surfing. Being in the ocean and riding waves is very healing and necessary for the well-being of my spirit.

Undoubtedly, it was a long hard road full of resistance. It all stems from the days when I used to primarily surf Trestles. Those were my training grounds where I learned the art of snaking and how to take-off deep. Eventually, I got tired of all the whining and hassling. Consequently, I figured the only way I was going to get waves alone was not only take-off deeper but to go faster.

In the next few chapters, I'm going to share with you some of the wave catching techniques that I've developed over the years. For the most part, some of them were fairly devious, but that's how it was. If nothing else, they make for some good stories!

*Judging Criteria: The surfer who catches the biggest best waves, doing the most radically controlled maneuvers, in the most critical section of the wave, with style and power throughout, for the longest functional distance, is deemed the winner.

4 - TAKE OFF DEEPER AND GO FASTER

Eventually, I improved enough to start taking off deeper than some of the boys. That didn't do much good though. They would drop-in on me anyhow. On top of that, the guys would cut back and push me off of the waves. This was so they could surf the rest of the wave alone. You'd think it would be embarrassing to drop in on a chick and then push her off, but they thought this was funny and just laughed.

After all the struggling with the boys to get waves, I finally told myself that if didn't want them to burn me I'd not only have to take-off deeper, I'd have to go faster too. The fact is, no one in their right mind is going to drop in on someone flying down the line at Mach speed without risking a serious injury. Speed is the key to high-performance surfing anyway. On the positive side, all of this harassment helped improve my surfing skills. Indeed, it wasn't long before I started getting more quality waves to myself!

Eventually, it became increasingly difficult for them to get waves from me. Now, they'd have to come up with some new antics, and they did. Such as, when I'd be taking off they'd pull my leash to keep me out of a wave. This in turn, also helped them launch themselves into the waves. They continued burning me every opportunity they could. Many times this would continue into the next session, or like I said earlier it could resume the next day or even the following week. Really, if we were all going to continue surfing at Trestles, it'd be in everyone's best interest to just get along. Well, at least quit snaking each other. No doubt, we all preferred to ride waves alone anyhow!

The primary change came during one of the local crew's annual Memorial Day parties at the shack. What I loved most about these parties was the boys would get too drunk to surf! This is when I'd have a wave-fest, by taking advantage of the uncrowded surf while they were in a drunken stupor! Finally, at one of these parties, I brought a peace offering. With a sly grin on my face, I walked up to the guys with a big batch of "special" homemade brownies. Don't get me wrong they ate them willingly, knowing they were laced with marijuana. This guaranteed they'd be too drunk *and* stoned to surf. For sure this was by far my most devious scheme yet! Waiting until the boys at the shack were half-crocked, and hopefully more receptive, I let them know there was something I wanted to say. Their initial reaction despite their demeanor and the delicious tray of brownies was *"Ugh, what does she want now?"* I told them I wanted to thank them for all the years that they'd hassled me. They helped me become a better surfer and prepared me for any type of lineup. Some of them were really good surfers too. I learned from watching the ones that ripped, even if I didn't particularly like them. After my announcement, they started applauding and offered me a beer – Which I gratefully accepted. After that, we all got along much better. Well, most of us that is – The exception was *Danger Duck*.

During my first pregnancy, the guy we called *Danger Duck*, obnoxious as usual, did his best to capitalize on my pregnant condition. While I was patiently waiting for a wave, trying to be cautious, this beauty rolls in right towards me. I started paddling for it when *Danger Duck* frantically paddled over as hard as he could to get beneath me. He blocked it so that I couldn't take-off. Another way of snaking someone! Due to the fact that I was seven months pregnant, I backed off and let him go without a hassle. Normally I would've paddled right over him. Well, after all that he ended up missing the wave! This left me in the perfect position for the next wave. This wave was even better than the previous one! I was so stoked to have no one around to hustle me this time, or so I thought. Casually, I started stroking into the wave when *Danger Duck* whipped his board around and paddled underneath me again! He was trying to intimidate me into not going. Throwing caution to the wind I thought, "Screw that! I'm going!" Immediately I redirected the angle of my board to take-off deeper, and to prevent from running him over.

This time I called him off of the wave, but *Danger Duck ignored me* and dropped in anyhow. He surfed right in front of me while I yelled: "*Come on dude, kick out!*" He didn't. Asking him again, he still wouldn't get out of the way. Being that this was a right-hand wave, and he is a regular footer, he was facing the wave. I'm a goofy footer so my back's to the wave. This put us back to back. He was riding his short board, but I was on my longboard, which enabled me to go faster. As a result, every time I came off the bottom of the wave I instantly caught up to him. Asking him for the third time to kick out, it was obvious he still had no intention of doing so. I wasn't going to ask again. For that reason, I planned to edge him out over the top of the wave. What happened instead, was he ended up sitting totally balanced on my back while I was in a squatted position. This situation required that I make a split-second decision. Knowing that I should be careful, after all, I was pregnant, I just couldn't help myself. This set up was too perfect to pass up. Hence, I quickly stood up in one thrusting motion. This literally flung him into the air, flipping him head over heels with the lip of the wave, tossing him over the falls. Somehow, I stayed on my board and came flying back down the wave through a cascade of white water. Emerging with a tremendous amount of speed, I had a huge smile on my face. From there, I cranked a hard bottom turn that projected me down the line across the wave. This is when I gave out a loud hoot and claimed the wave raising both arms above my head victoriously. Over the sound of the surf, I could hear the roar of laughter and screaming coming from the boys on the beach too. Continuing to ride the wave, I carved it all the way to shore. Surprisingly, I got a standing ovation from the boys at the shack! Another classic moment in the adventures of *Danger Woman!*

Humiliated, *Danger Duck* had been humbled by a pregnant woman he tried to stuff. He was teased and ridicule mercilessly by his peers. Instant Karma dude! Thirty years later, we occasionally end up surfing Upper Trestles at the same time. He *still* gives me stink eye with a scowl on his face, and I still smile at the memory.

These were the formative days of surfing that taught me to be as ruthless in the water as the boys. This is also what forced me to be increasingly imaginative with my own wave catching strategies. Of course, it'd be best to apply them when I wasn't pregnant. Meanwhile, surfing pregnant was my way of riding tandem!

5 - GOING TANDEM

All of my kids have surfed since they were negative nine - months old. It appeared that surfing with a pregnant woman in the lineup terrified most guys and kept them at a safe distance (this is one way of catching more waves)! At some point, that little voice in my head would tell me when it was time to take a break from surfing. Intuitively, I'd stop surfing sometime after the seventh month but before the ninth month. The best part about surfing pregnant was that it helped me do some of the hardest cutbacks of my life! After gathering as much speed and momentum as possible, I'd stick out my belly as I started going into a turn. From there I used the weight to let the centrifugal force swing me around into a full roundhouse cutback. This involved very little effort, giving me a tremendous amount of power.

Other than that, the biggest difference I felt when I was surfing pregnant was that I tired quickly. I couldn't surf for twelve hours anymore! Sadly, I was only good for three. Likewise, the only time I felt uncomfortable surfing pregnant was between the fourth and fifth months (beginning of the second trimester). Unfortunately, I tended to cramp up after a couple hours of surfing. Embarrassed, I'd have to ask the lifeguards (at Trestles) for a ride back up to the top of the trail. The lifeguards would reluctantly give me a ride out, shake their heads, and beg me not to surf anymore until after I had the kid! Of course, I'd be back the following week hoping I was past the cramping stage and wouldn't have to ask for another ride. If you've never been to Trestles, you'll find that it's quite a hike. Especially on the walk out when you're surfed out, pregnant, and hauling a couple of little kids in a wagon. This included all their toys, diapers, extra clothes, soaking wet wetsuits, surfboards, etc.

At first, the guys were stoked that I was pregnant. Not because they were happy for me, but because they knew I'd be out of the lineup for a while. Nevertheless, that wasn't the case. When I was pregnant with my first kid I was out surfing, waiting for a set, when my wetsuit zipper blew out from all the stress on it. The guys started laughing and clapping. They were probably thinking I'd be out of the water for sure now. Instead of giving up I paddled in and struggled out of my wetsuit (no easy task with the zipper stuck half ways down). Without delay, I put my husband's wetsuit on and paddled right back out. Being that it was kinda big, his wetsuit barely fit me but it was good enough. Besides, there was room to grow into it and continue surfing for a few more months. That was all I needed!

During my second pregnancy, I scored some of the biggest, best Rincon I've ever seen! There were some solid twenty-foot waves with excellent shape! My husband was begging me not to go out there. In response, I was begging him to come surfing with me. He was worried, but I wasn't concerned. The truth is, I was stoked! My doctor told me the fetus was well protected until the last trimester (I was only a couple of months pregnant). In any event, I paddle out alone (other than the baby in my tummy)!

Carefully timing the sets, I paddled out at the river mouth. From there I moved up to Indicators, which is the furthest point out. When the surf is this big, wave selection becomes crucial. Choosing the largest waves enabled me to ride further down the beach because all the sections connected. I was kicking out past the freeway onramp. Believe me, that's a really long ride! Consequently, I had to scramble up the rocks with my surfboard while avoiding the crashing waves. Then I had to walk along the freeway to get back to the beach. Although I only rode four waves that morning, it was better than riding a dozen mediocre ones. Unbelievably, no one dropped in on any of my rides! This is rare at such a crowded point break like Rincon. Then again, when it's that big it helps keep the crowds down.

When I was more than five months pregnant with my third kid, I visited the North Shore of Oahu, Hawaii. Intentionally, I went in late May, during the off-season, hoping the waves wouldn't be too big nor tempting. Further, I wanted to go before I got too big! However, there were a few good double overhead swells that I couldn't resist. What's more, the Hawaiians were super cool towards me. They kept encouraging me to surf the waves with them. The boys loved surfing with me. Laughing, they said it fascinated them to watch a pregnant woman rip. They really got a kick out of this. I got plenty of waves, too! When I returned to Hawaii the following season, the guys in the surf asked me, "Well sista, wat is it? Wat you have?" Looking at them in wonder I said, "What are you talking about?" They replied, "Da baby, sista? Is it a boy or a girl?" Smiling, I said it was a baby girl named Margeaux. She was named after Margo Godfrey Oberg, a world champion surfer from the 70's. Albeit, I spelled her name differently, it was still in hopes of her becoming an excellent surfer. No doubt, I wasn't disappointed! Margeaux is a world-class surfer (and a U.S.A. nose-riding Champion). I must admit, it was surprising how many of da boyz remembered me from the year before. I guess charging

Hawaiian surf while several months pregnant is one way to get a name on the North Shore!

When most people found out that I surfed during my pregnancies, the first thing they'd ask was for how long. I would say, "Until my fingertips no longer reached the water while paddling!" Although it's still uncommon to see pregnant women surfing, it was unheard of back in the day. Like I said, most guys were scared to death to surf near a pregnant woman and kept a safe distance. By the way, this technique is specifically for women who are already pregnant. In other words, don't get pregnant simply so you can get more waves! Keep in mind, once you have a baby your surfing time will be very limited (at least for a while).

Years later (after having babies), I purposely put on a few extra pounds trying to see if I could surf as powerful as when I was pregnant. This was in hopes that the extra fat would help me stay warmer too, but it didn't work. My belly must've been perfectly centered when I was pregnant. Regrettably, this experiment was a failure and I ended up having to lose the weight, and then work hard to get back into shape.

Take into account, that regardless of which wave catching techniques you plan on using, it's imperative that you're a competent paddler first. The better you are at paddling, the more waves you will catch!

6 - THE PADDLER

When it comes to riding waves I'm not very particular. Of course, I love perfect surf, but really I'll ride just about anything. Over the years I've surfed waves that were so small and crappy that there'd be no one else surfing for as far as I could see. Yet, for some reason, there was always some dude who'd paddle out and sit right next to me. Not only that, then he'd start hustling me for waves. Honestly, I used to think I was cursed! It was so predictable that my friends and I would joke about it, but I really didn't find it very funny. Sometimes I just want to surf a few waves alone, peacefully.

I've handled this situation several different ways. Once, I asked this guy if he could please paddle down the beach. I told the intruder that my girlfriends and I were grieving the death of a dear friend and needed some privacy. One of my lines was asking guys if they'd assist me with a college project. The subject was a sociological study on: "Why people crowd other people when there's an abundance of open space available?" I've experienced this both in the water and on the beach for years. I call it the "crowd mentality". Mostly, I was curious what their answer would be. One time when I asked this guy if he'd help me with the school project, he asked if I wanted him to tell me the truth? "Of course!" I said, "Why else would I ask?" This is when he admitted that he was afraid to be out in the ocean alone. What can you say when a grown man admits this to a woman? All I could say was, "Okay, then let's surf some waves together." He was stoked and said I could have any wave I wanted. Really folks, please learn how to find your own lineup. And, if you're scared to surf alone then bring a friend along.

The one incident that sticks out the most was the time I conned this guy into paddling until he was exhausted. This happened on a small blown out afternoon while my friend and I were surfing at Bolsa Chica. The only reason it was fun was because we were alone. In reality, the waves sucked. Of course, our solo session didn't last very long. For soon enough this guy (from now on called *The Paddler*), came out and sat right next to me. Not next to my friend, but me! Is this because I'm a girl? This guy sat so close to me I could hardly spin my board around to catch a wave. When the first little ripple came dribbling in (one could barely call it a wave), he scrambled around me and took it. After his ride, he paddled back out, zipped around me, and immediately took another wave. After the third time, I had enough. Three strikes and you're out! Now I was perturbed. I asked my friend "Is this guy for real? Watch what I'm going to do the next time he attempts to take another wave from me." He saw a big smile on my face and said, "Oh no, what're you going to do this time?" My friend had no idea what I might do next. One thing for sure, he knew it'd be something amusing! It was no sooner said, when this bonehead started to paddle around me, trying to snake me again. This time I was ready! Keep in mind the waves were so tiny that it'd be more entertaining to play games with him than surf.

I waited until he was about to paddle past me before I started paddling. Beginning slowly at first, I then built up some momentum staying slightly ahead of him so he couldn't get on the other side of me. Each time *The Paddler* thought he was going to pass me I'd picked up the pace. I kept on paddling. At one point, I was far enough ahead of him to stop for a moment until he caught up. I lured him on by sitting up on my board like I was waiting for a wave. When he arrived and started to paddle past me, I laid down and started paddling again. This was done on purpose so he wouldn't have time to rest. He so desperately didn't want me to sit deeper than him, that he kept on following me. Having fun, I kept him paddling. It was like *running* a fish until it was tired.

Finally, I let him paddle past me and waited until he sat up on his board. Again, he must've thought he was going to get a break. However, I had something else in mind. When it looked as though I was going to pass him, he started paddling again. Sorry dude, no rest for the weary! I continued to follow him until he couldn't take another stroke. Me, I was just warming up! One of the ways I trained for big waves was going for long paddles. Likewise, no matter what size the surf is I paddle hard to stay fit. Therefore, for me paddling is like taking a walk in the park.

By now we were so far up the beach I could barely see my friend. We had paddled for at least a quarter of a mile when out of pure exhaustion, *The Paddler* was forced to stop and rest. This time, I passed him and sat smack next to him like he had done to me earlier. After riding the first wave, I hauled ass back out. The moment he realized I was going around him, he started trying to paddle again, but by then he had a bad case of spaghetti arms. He could barely take a few strokes before he'd have to stop and rest again. The next time, I paddled around him and sat even closer. We were almost bumping shoulders. It was hard for me to keep a straight face and not laugh. This was ridiculous we hadn't said one word to each other. I'd have to say, testing out my new theory (to paddle someone to the point of exhaustion), was not only entertaining but it was working!

The waves were still sloppy little peaks breaking all over the place. There was no dominant wave direction and you could easily surf to the right or left. It was obvious by the way he'd snagged the first few waves from me that he preferred to go left. This made the game even easier because I knew which way he wanted to go. *The Paddler* was a goofy-footer and apparently more comfortable surfing front-side. This isn't uncommon. Trust me, it's in your best interest to know how to surf competently in both directions. By doing so, you can increase your opportunity to get fifty percent more waves!

To resume, by now it was darn near impossible for this guy to get a wave unless I was already riding one or paddling back out. He finally gave up and went in. He was too tired to paddle for a wave, let alone out position me for one. Pathetically, he didn't even surf in! All he could do was let the whitewater push him towards the beach. By the way, this is another unwritten rule (or what's considered part of the surfer's code); you always ride your last wave in (unless you arrived by boat)! Also, there's no going in after a wipeout either (unless you are injured).

When *The Paddler* (one tired out dude), finally reached the shore, he had a long walk back to where we'd originally started. I surfed a series of lefts back down the beach to where my friend was still surfing alone. Not surprisingly, I arrived there quicker than the time it took this guy to walk the same distance. It was fascinating to see to what extreme some guys will let their egos take them.

Subsequently, after trying out a new wave catching strategy, I put it to the test. Once it's proven an effective method, I then add it to my repertoire. In truth, most of the wave-catching tricks I use are based on the guy's egos. The thing is you poor boys can't help yourselves. As a result, it enables us, girls, to catch more waves! Thanks, and please take no offense, it just is. In any event, seeing how *The Paddler's* ego made him keep paddling, it had me thinking of other ways to capitalize on the boys (and yes, occasionally the girls) egos. It didn't take long to figure this out. The first thing I thought of was what happens when the cameras come out!

7 - THE PHOTO SHOOT

If there's one thing all surfers love, it's a good photo of themselves surfing. Sad to say, I've seen uncrowded surf get packed with surfers the moment the photographers show up with their cameras. There are some spots known for having photographers on location anytime there is decent surf. These are the breaks that have a consistent combination of talented surfers and good waves, making it easy to get good photos. These are the spots I prefer to avoid. The crowds are too intense and filled with egomaniacs, all hoping to get their photos in the magazines. With this in mind, I thought I'd experiment and see if using a camera could help me get more waves. This turned out to be another successful wave catching technique. With modern technology, this may be somewhat antiquated, but with a little creativity, you could still incorporate it into your bag of tricks.

First, get a water camera and take it out surfing with you. Next, start off by swimming out and taking photos of your friends surfing. If it's shallow enough you can stand on the inside. If you're in deeper water, where there are strong currents or you need to cover a larger area, wear swim fins. A word of caution: Stay out of the way of surfers riding waves and watch out for loose surfboards. There's no doubt people will notice you taking photos. If you see someone getting a good ride take a shot of them too. Most likely, they'll ask you to send them a copy.

After a while go in and get your board and then paddle back out with the camera. This way you can take pictures of people surfing while you are both riding the same wave. Ask your friend to surf in front of you on a few waves so you can take some shots. Then let some of the other surfers go in front of you and take photos of them too. Next, ask one of them if you can take off in front of them so you can get a different angle. If they agree, then during the ride turn around and snap some shots of them. Keep in mind, for this trick you have to be able to surf facing backwards while taking a photo. Be extra aware of your surroundings and look far ahead before turning around. This is to make sure there are no surfers or swimmers in your path. Soon enough, you can have just about any wave you want from the surfers you've been photographing. No one will complain. Why? Because everyone likes a photo of themselves surfing!

I've taken some classic photos of my daughter Margeaux. She has a beautiful style and spends most of the time perched on the nose of her vintage longboard. The way she surfs so effortlessly across the waves makes taking good photos of her easy. No doubt, she is the youngest surfing master I know. My definition of a master is someone who uses the least amount of effort for the most effectiveness. These are the people who make something that's very difficult look easy.

On one of our mini surf adventures to Malibu, I was taking photos of Margeaux and her friends surfing. When this guy noticed what we were doing he asked if I'd take some photos of him too. He said he didn't have any pictures of himself surfing and would really like some. He was so stoked when I agreed. After this, every time he caught a wave he encouraged me to ride in front of him in hopes of getting some good photos. Really I had good intentions, but on the first wave, I realized that my camera was out of film. Unfortunately, I didn't have any more disposable water cameras left. If I had, I would've gone in and grabbed one.

Needless to say, I should've told him right away, but instead, I continued surfing in front of him pretending to take photos. The waves were super fun but it was really crowded. I was just being lazy and didn't want to deal with having to hustle with the other surfers. To make myself feel better I let him go in front of me a few times too. Without question, I wouldn't have had half as many rides if it weren't for faking the photos of that poor guy (and a few others). This was a terrible excuse to get more waves, but I just couldn't resist. Yet, I bet it was something Miki Dora would've appreciated. He was ruthless in the surf with no regard for other surfers. Miki was surfing's most infamous rebel.

When I got out of the water the guy followed me in to make sure he could get a copy of the photos (which wasn't surprising). Yet, I still didn't have the heart to tell him that I'd been out of film. While he was giving me his contact information, I couldn't even look him in the eye. Moreover, my daughter was aware of what I had done and was disappointed. This made me feel even worse. What a horrible example I was setting. She was always encouraging me to do the right thing. Likewise, I was hoping that this guy wouldn't recognize me in any magazines or on television. Despite the fact I caught plenty of waves that day, I must admit I felt guilty taking advantage of him.

This experience could very well be a story about Karma because many years since that incident, I've had numerous photo shoots go wrong. For example, the film would run out after I only caught a few waves, if any. On several occasions, the camera operator would be looking the other way on one of my best rides of the day. Another time, a professional photographer brought the body of her camera but forgot the lenses. This was for a scheduled photo shoot way up north. Actually, I was grateful I hadn't paddled out first. No one else was out, the waves were only mediocre, the water was freezing cold and it was not uncommon to see sharks. Not to mention, while we were standing there checking out the surf, a huge mother whale and her calf swam directly through the surf line. This is where I would've been surfing! Maybe this was good Karma? Now the photographer was twice as bummed! She missed the *photo-op* with me, *and* the whales (probably more for missing the whales). I must admit surfing some of those Northern California breaks alone can be quite unnerving.

Oh, and then there was the time that I was so excited to get photos taken in good surf, that I forgot to put the fin in my longboard! Sure enough, on the first turn, the board slid out from under me causing me to eat it, while my board washed to shore. Although I'd suspected what had happened, it wasn't until after swimming in that it was confirmed. This made me laugh! With the surf so good, and the photographer waiting, I wanted to hurry. This entailed running across the sand and going back up several flights of stairs to where my van was parked. Then I had to dig the key out of the hidden pocket in my wetsuit. Hastily, I unlocked the van, grabbed my fin, locked the van back up, and then stuffed the key back into my wetsuit.

Fin in hand, I stopped at the top of the cliff to take a quick survey of the waves. That's when I noticed the surf conditions had drastically changed for the worse. How fast things can change! The waves that were previously about four to five feet high, with clean glassy peaks, had deteriorated. Regrettably, the strong onshore winds had instantly destroyed the surf, transforming it into blown out choppy junk. Shattered, I wasn't laughing now. Damn it, the photo shoot that I'd just driven all the way to San Diego from Huntington for had to be aborted!

It's unfortunate that very few of my biggest waves have been documented throughout the years. The one year I entered the XXL Big

Wave event (2005), I caught one of the biggest waves of my life at Waimea Bay. It was late in the season when a huge, clean swell hit The Bay full force. Purely by chance, I was staying right across the street in Waimea Valley. My friends had invited me to share a tiny room (10' x 10') they were renting at the three-story wooden house that's nestled next to the cliff. This is directly below the sacred Heiau, Puu o Mahuka (the largest Heiau on Oahu). When I first arrived, I was guided to go up there and make an offering to the ancient Hawaiian ancestors in exchange for their blessings. This had to be done *before* I surfed. Knowing this, I went that evening (so spooky). This was because I wanted to surf first thing in the morning! In return, the *Spirits* granted me permission to surf the beautiful waves of Hawaii. With their blessings, my safety was assured. In gratitude, I took offerings up there a few times for protecting me in the giant surf. Besides, it was an ideal location for a surf check of The Bay. Also, the view of the coastline, that included Ka'ena Point, which was breathtaking.

After I had been there for a couple of weeks, I was woken up in the middle of the night by the sound of pounding surf. Amazingly, this powerful swell shook the entire house! Quietly slipping out of the room, so I wouldn't wake up my friends, I went outside onto the deck to check it out. Stunned, I couldn't believe my eyes! There were huge sets of waves thundering in! It was so awesome to watch, especially with the moon lighting up the ocean. I thought, *here it is! Tomorrow is the day I've been waiting for my entire life. The waves I've dreamed of surfing since I was a little girl.* There was no doubt it'd be some of the biggest surf I'd ever been in. It was really big! It was hard to go back to sleep after that. Every time I shut my eyes I kept seeing those huge waves breaking over and over in my head. The house continued to shake every time a wave broke. That didn't help my nerves much either.

The moment it was light I jumped out of bed. Running up the stairs to my lookout spot on the deck, I noticed that the surf was even bigger and the swell was still building. Holy crap! The wave faces were close to thirty feet or more, on some of the biggest sets. I was so psyched up

I decided to skip having coffee. Hell, the thought of paddling out there alone made me jittery enough! Before I thought about it too much, I threw my bathing suit on, grabbed my ten-foot rhino chaser, a bar of wax and headed across the street to the beach. With the board tucked tightly under my arm, I started praying. Admittedly, I also asked for the spirit of the legendary Hawaiian surfer, *Eddie Aikau, to keep an eye on me while I was out surfing Waimea Bay.

Once I was on the beach, I waxed my board and then started stretching while carefully studying the surf. Not only did I time the sets and watch how the patterns of the waves were breaking, I closely observed how, and where, the guys were paddling out too. On one hand, I thought it'd be wise to paddle out the same way I saw all the guys doing it. Yet, I was very uncomfortable with their technique. What they'd do was, run down the beach and jump into the receding water from the previous wave that had just washed up the beach. Then they'd slide under the next approaching wave right before it slammed on the shore. It was so shallow that if by chance your fins happen to get stuck in the sand, you'd be left directly in the impact zone of the infamous Waimea shore break. In other words, you were screwed.

It was about an hour before I finally got the courage to go for it. When I did paddle out I decided to do it my own way. I've never been let down using my own intuition, but I've sure paid when I didn't listen! With precise timing and a helluva lot of paddling, I made it safely out to the lineup (glad I listened to myself). What a thrill! It was so exhilarating and absolutely magnificent just being out there. The bright sunlight, combined with the howling offshore winds, created beautiful rainbows in the spray that was blowing off the tops of the waves. With the spectacular view of Waimea Valley as a backdrop, it doesn't get much better than this.

With that in mind, I figured if I was going to die anywhere, I couldn't think of a better place. On the contrary, I ended up having an epic session and caught some incredible waves that day. Honestly, there's nothing in the world I've ever experienced that's like dropping in over the ledge of a huge wave! Definitely, it's that moment of total commitment '*Do or die*'. Surfing is excellent for being *in the moment*.

The first ride helped me get rid of the jitters. After each consecutive ride, I worked my way further into the lineup, taking off deeper and deeper. After a while, I was pushing my personal limits and looking for the biggest wave I could ride. This was no easy feat with more than forty guys out (no women) with the same thing in mind: to catch the biggest wave you can and survive! After about three rides, I found myself positioned for a humongous wave! To my amazement, it lurched up about thirty-five feet or higher! This was the wave I was waiting for! Catching it with no one else on it was unbelievable! This is rare in big crowded surf. In a big wave setting most waves have at least a few guys on them. This is because once you commit it's more dangerous to pull out than to keep going. The waves themselves were scary enough. When you added all the surfers and the winds blowing abandoned boards around, it becomes downright treacherous! I was psyched!

Nonetheless, I started counting strokes and taking big breaths to stay calm as I paddled into the wave. It felt like I was paddling forever! I wanted to make absolutely sure I was into the wave before I stood up. There was so much power and energy emanating from that wave it felt like it was creating an electrical charge in the atmosphere. I think every cell in my body was on alert! The hard offshore winds were stinging my eyes as well as trying to blow me out the back of the wave. Simultaneously, there was so much water draining off of the reef that it was threatening to suck me back up the face of the wave. Hell, I barely weighed enough to keep my board in the wave! Not being able to see, I had to rely on feeling my way down the face of the wave.

Somehow, I negotiated the double airdrop with my toes barely connected to the board. When I finally made it to the bottom and opened my eyes, I was dangerously low on the wave. Suddenly, it was apparent that if I had any chance of making it all, I'd have to get higher up the face of the wave immediately. Instinctively, I cranked a hard, long, drawn out turn. A *ginormous* wall of water was already pitching towards the sky threatening to pummel me to death! If I failed to escape this heaving monster, it was going to feel like the entire ocean landing on me! Aiming high I made the section and started racing across the wind-rippled face. Under the circumstances, it took every bit of skill I had accumulated over the years to keep my nerve and prevent me from jumping off my board out of sheer fright! After pumping a few more turns that shot me down the line, I was rewarded by making it to the deeper waters of the bay where the waves back-off.

This was one of my greatest surfing moments ever! Grinning from ear to ear, I paddled back out for a few more, but it was unlikely I'd catch another wave that big or good, especially alone. Regardless, I thought I'd try. After a couple more fun rides I made it happily back to the beach unscathed. The last wave I rode took me all the way to shore. Literally, I stepped off my board onto the sand, safe once again! If it weren't for the wind blowing off the tops of the waves, it would've been a dry-haired session. Thank God I didn't have to negotiate the deadly Waimea shore break! Or worse yet, experience a hideous wipeout with a long hold down (thanks, Eddie). This truly was an epic dream session!

As I was walking up the beach some guy came running up to compliment me on my rides. He told me how he'd captured my biggest wave on video. Already stoked, now I was ecstatic! Honestly, I couldn't believe my stroke of good luck! Immediately, I asked him for a copy of the video. Excited, I shared with him how I'd entered the yearlong *XXL Big Wave Competition* during the last month of the event. This was in hopes of winning the women's division. In addition, with a copy of the footage, I could win five thousand dollars! Likewise, he could win a thousand. He said, "No problem, I'll make a copy for you." We then exchanged phone numbers. However, every time I called him he said he hadn't made a copy yet. Since the deadline to submit the footage for the *XXL* was coming up, I continued to pester him every few days. Finally, I even offered to split the prize money with him! Still, he never did provide me with a copy of the video. I've no doubt I would've won the event if I could've obtained the required footage. I placed second.

Although I've had some great photos taken of me surfing big Puerto Escondido, the magazines consistently rejected them. Even when I won the world championships, a magnifying glass was needed to see the photo they printed of me surfing (at least they printed one)! During the last year before retiring, I got quite a few photos in the magazines. The thing is, they weren't shots of me surfing, but holding up first-place trophies. It's possible that this was my bad Karma for not being honest with that poor surfer at Malibu. Overall, I've had incredibly good luck (or good Karma) by being blessed with an abundance of excellent waves throughout the years, regardless of the lack of photos.

*Eddie Aikua - Eddie was one of the very best big wave riders, and the first professional lifeguard at Waimea Bay on the North Shore of Oahu, Hawaii. It helped that Waimea was his favorite surf spot and he was totally in tune with it. He was (and always will be) a highly respected waterman who constantly risked his life to rescue others. Amazingly, he had a perfect record of saving over five hundred people with no drownings.

In 1978, when he was thirty-one years old, Eddie volunteered as an honorable crewmember on the prestigious Hokule'a. This was a double-hulled voyaging canoe that was making a second attempt to follow the ancient Polynesian route between the Tahitian and the Hawaiian Islands. Eddie was passionate about this voyage and trained very hard for it. Unfortunately, the day they were set to sail it was stormy and dangerous. With all the ongoing media and hoopla they must have felt pressured to embark. For against their better judgment they launched the ship anyway. Tragically, off the coast of Molokai, the ship started leaking and then capsized. After hanging on for so long the crew started to get exhausted. Also, they were at risk of suffering hypothermia from the exposure to the elements.

Eddie volunteered to paddle to Lanai, the closest island, to seek help for the rest of the crew. Reluctantly, the Captain finally allowed Eddie to go. At this point, the crew prayed that Eddie would make it to shore believing that otherwise, they'd perish. However, they ended up getting rescued – But Eddie was lost at sea. Although his board was later found after an extensive search, Eddie was never seen again. There are many of us who feel his spirit is still watching over all the surfers and swimmers at Waimea Bay.

8 - ANY WAVE YOU WANT BRO

Years ago, down deep in the jungles of mainland Mexico, a group of us girls went on a photo shoot for a surf magazine. Jim and his assistant were the photographers who were sent along with us. They were also surfers, but they were too busy filming us to surf themselves. They watched us get some great surf, wave after wave, day after day and one quality point break after another. We raced up and down the dirt roads off the main highway. Depending on the tides and winds, sometimes we surfed up to three different locations in a single day. The poor photographers had to pack and unpack their heavy equipment each time, and then lug all of it up and down the beach. They stood in the baking hot tropical sun for hours while we surfed the seasonally cooler waters of Mexico.

On the last day of the trip, we surfed the break that was closest to the hotel to lessen the risk of missing our flight back home. It's very easy to lose track of time while surfing. This was the first opportunity the photographers had to surf so they paddled out with us. Unfortunately, the waves were really small and blown out with funky rips. Honestly, I wasn't very stoked on this spot. It's no fun ending a surf trip in lousy waves. This surf break definitely had the poorest waves of the entire trip.

However, I noticed what appeared to be some great looking waves breaking about a half-mile out down the beach. I kept watching them and wanted to get a closer look. They looked very surfable to me. Could it really be as good as it looked so close to the crappy waves we were riding? I was trying to get someone to paddle down there with me. I'd already had a crocodile pop up right in front of me, and there were probably sharks too. So I figured if I was going to get chomped I might as well be in good surf. The guys volunteered to paddle down and check it out with me. All the girls, except for one, were too sketched out to paddle across the open waters of the bay with us. They thought it was too risky. I must admit, it was far from shore with lots of currents and who knows what else. The one girl who did go with us went in after her first wave. She couldn't wait to get out of the water. There was too much sea life for her liking. As a result, she chose a long difficult hike as opposed to paddling back.

I couldn't believe how good it was! The way the coast curved made it so the winds were hitting the waves offshore. This was primarily a left that started out in deep water, then broke for several hundred yards continuing past a river mouth. No wonder there was so much fish activity in the water! River mouths are usually murky and known as prime feeding grounds. In other words, they are notorious for attracting sharks!

Out here the swells were a solid eight-foot with the wave faces being about ten to eleven feet high. No doubt, this was one of the most playful waves I've ever ridden! The deeper water caused the wave to be really slow and mushy which made it easy to take-off. On the outside, huge maneuvers could be done fearlessly as if the waves were only two to three feet. Then the waves would hit the inside sandbars and gain momentum as they approached the river mouth. As a result, this caused them to jack-up and start grinding down the beach getting bigger, faster and steeper (most point waves get smaller as they peel into a bay). Which in turn, enabled you to start racing down the line at mach-speed. This is a good thing too because you'd need all that speed to backdoor the next hollow pitching section. If you made it through the tube, the wave would spit you out at the other end. You just had to be sure to kick out in time before the heavy shore-break slammed you onto the rocky beach. Other than that, the only real downfall was the long paddle back out through the critter-filled waters!

Needless to say, I'd just surfed my butt off for the past week and now it was their turn. To show my appreciation for the hard work these photographers had been doing, I told them they could have any wave they wanted. First of all, it's known by most surfers not to take off on the first wave of the set. Let it slide by unridden. If you do paddle for the first wave and miss it, there's a good chance you'll be too far in and get caught by the rest of the set. This can be serious in bigger surf. Besides, the first wave is usually smaller and less powerful. Remember, the ocean has many moods and is very unpredictable. This is why I always encourage my students to study the surf conditions before they paddle out. Yet still, the conditions are subject to change at any moment and sometimes they change very quickly.

With that being said, I decided to take the first wave, ride the beef of it and then kick out early. This was done in hopes of catching a second wave before the set was over (I do this quite often to get more waves). Well, it just so happened that on this swell the first wave was consistently the best wave of the set. There were several waves per set so I easily got my quota of two waves per set even after a long ride. After doing this several times, the guys decided they wanted the first wave. I said, "Go ahead, catch any wave you want. Take the first one, the second one, I don't care, it doesn't matter to me. When the next set came in they started hustling each other and arguing over who was going to get the first wave. They ended up both paddling into it taking off side by side, riding the wave together. Then they started play fighting trying to push each other off until they both ended up falling. It was especially entertaining watching them fight over that wave since there were plenty of waves for all of us to ride. And, we were the only ones out!

On this particular set, the second wave happened to be the wave of the day. What luck! I was so stoked I didn't have to give up this wave to one of them. With only a few strokes, I glided into the wave dropping in effortlessly on a solid ten-footer. After cranking a hard bottom turn that shot me straight up, I smacked the lip and did a reentry that set me up for another bottom turn. This next turn launched me far out onto the shoulder where I got really low, grabbed the rail, and went into a huge roundhouse cutback. I literally surfed a circle around the boys, who were scrambling to get back up onto their boards. From there, I banked off of the foam ball and flew back past them. This was done with a big shit-eating grin. I could hear them razzing me for tricking them.

Continuing my ride, I surfed across the river mouth racing the hollow inside section. When the wave started to pitch I quickly slipped under the lip and pulled into a thick barrel that was breaking in extremely shallow water. I could hear the rocks tumbling under me, and the gravelly sand hitting the bottom of my board. I was totally locked-in with no way out. There was no option but to make it or get bounced on the rocks. Riding high, I made it through the tube getting spit out the other end. After that, the wave was still reeling down the beach but it was breaking dangerously close to the shore. Yet, I kept on going as far as I dared! Finally, I decided I'd pushed my luck far enough and I'd better kick out. I wasn't wearing a leash and didn't want my board to get crushed, or have to scramble over the rocks to retrieve it. Oh yeah, I didn't want to get hurt either! At that stage, I was way down the beach where the jungle was dense with who knows what might be lurking nearby! I made sure I stayed with my board.

It was a long paddle just to get back past the river mouth and an even longer paddle out to the lineup. Fish were jumping out of the ocean all around me. Obviously, they were being chased by something bigger that I couldn't see. This is the time to paddle very gently with your hands barely skimming the surface. The last thing you want to do is make too many splashes attracting attention to yourself.

When I was about halfway back to the lineup I could sense something watching me. I was starting to get spooked. Continuing to paddle gently I kept looking around. Now I was pretty sure I was being followed, but by what I had no idea. Finally, I saw that it was a little sea lion. He kept on following me and it started to make me feel a bit nervous. As cute as they are, sea lions can be very territorial. We were surfing in a semi-isolated spot and I wasn't even close to where the other two surfers were. Also, I was quite a ways from shore now too. The sea lion continued to swim around me poking his head up here and there. I wasn't sure where he was going to pop up next. As he got closer I realized that he wasn't so little after all! If you've ever been around one of these animals you'll notice that their small heads are way out of proportion to the rest of their bodies. I should've known better!

What seemed like an awfully long time, I finally made it back out to where the guys were. The sea lion continued to hang around wherever I went. For some reason, he didn't seem too interested in the guys. Whenever I took off on a wave, the sea lion would catch the wave and surf it with me. Riding the wave for only a short distance he'd then dive under as I continued my ride. When I paddled back out he'd be there waiting for me. He did this for a few sets then finally swam off. I guess he was just curious!

Anyhow, the guys started teasing me about conning them into going on that first wave. Laughing, I reminded them that I'd given them their choice of any wave they wanted. To this day they still think that I suckered them into it. I wish I was that powerful to control the surf! They laughed and said they had fun trying to push each other off on their wave. Hands down this was the biggest and best surf of the entire trip! They admitted wishing they'd caught a wave like the one I'd gotten, but they did catch some good ones themselves. They were also bummed they didn't have their cameras with them to capture my ride. Me too! This was probably karma from that damn Malibu photo scheme again! Oh well, having good wave karma is better than good photo karma any day! I still can't believe the girls didn't paddle over and surf with us. Especially after seeing us catch one great ride after another. Who knows? Fine with me, more waves for us.

Another time I remember was when I was driving up and down the coast with one of my surfing buddies. It was one of those crisp clear California days when everything is bright and glowing. We were on a wave-chasing mission. We checked out every surf spot we could think of. The problem was the waves were flat. We weren't searching for good surf, but for *any* surf. Not seeing a single soul out surfing or a breaking wave, we finally ended up at one of the jetties in Newport Beach. This was the only place a piddly wave was even close to breaking. It was so small and inconsistent that my friend chose not to paddle out. Seriously, when it did break it was max one-foot with an occasional two-footer at best. There was one guy out that already made it too crowded for a wave that was barely ridable. Two people out would make it packed, and three would be ludicrous.

Being that I was in one of my moods to surf no matter what, I paddled out anyway. I must admit, I was stoked my friend stayed on the beach! There's no doubt that guy was bummed to see me paddle out, let alone sit right next to him (this is taboo in surfing etiquette). Immediately I started apologizing: "Hey dude, I'm so sorry. Everywhere else we looked was totally flat. You can have any wave you want bro. Honestly, I just really wanted to surf today and only need a few waves." Out of respect, I made sure I didn't sit in the inside position. After that, he relaxed and knew he could have the first choice of any wave. During the lulls, we enjoyed swapping surf stories. When the sets did come, there were only two or three waves at a time. After the long wait, the guy would paddle feverishly for the first wave. I calmly waited for the next one, which would be predictably better. Every time he kicked out of a wave he'd see me on a better wave. After this happened several times he let out an audible, *"ARRGHHH"* of frustration as he slapped the water. He knew the second or third waves were usually the better ones, yet he still took the first wave every time. This happened for the entire session. *We even talked about it!* I offered to wait for the possible third wave or to take the first one. What can I say? I felt sorry for him but his ego kept getting the best of him. Surprisingly, I had a blast surfing that day. The only thing that I could think of to help him feel better was complimenting him on how well he rode those little waves. Compliments do work wonders!

9 - THE COMPLIMENT

Although the 'compliment technique' works great in any type of surf, I've chosen the point break to demonstrate this method. This is because points tend to break more consistently in the same general area. They have fewer take-off zones than a beach break, making it more difficult to out position the other surfers for waves. Thus, wave catching strategies will require a different approach.

As usual, observe the waves and watch them closely. This should be done before you paddle out (and once you're out there). Identify as many take-off zones as possible. Time the sets. Ask yourself, do the bigger sets shift, or swing wide? Where are the best waves breaking? Are the smaller inside waves less crowded? Getting a feel for the ability of the surfers is equally helpful. Watch for where the experienced surfers are taking off. See who's catching the best waves. Note which surfers are catching the most waves. Some surfers can only surf in one direction, mostly frontside. (This doesn't apply at a point break but it's worth mentioning for future use). Also, try to avoid the more aggro surfers and the "snakes". Don't forget to look out for the kooks too!

You'll notice a few surfers that are sitting way on the outside, patiently waiting for the biggest waves. They catch fewer waves, but usually get the best waves of the day. Whereas, others prefer the inside surf zone where it breaks more often. The inside is good for catching lots of waves, but they'll be smaller and filled with mostly beginners. These inexperienced surfers are clueless regarding surf etiquette. Too often they'll drop in and go straight towards the beach, directly in front someone who's riding across the wave. This is known as doing the "Straight-Off-Adolph." On top of it, when this happens, their ride usually ends with them pearling. This is from not angling their board on the take-off (if someone pearls in front of you look out for their board flying back towards you). These are the same surfers who panic and toss their boards aside. Although surfing around novices makes catching waves easier, it also makes it much more dangerous. If you choose to surf on the inside with them, be patient and give them a couple of free tips: DO NOT TAKE OFF IN FRONT OF OTHER SURFERS! PLEASE LOOK BOTH WAYS BEFORE GOING! On the other hand, it wouldn't hurt to give them a couple of free waves along with their tips. While you're at it, you may suggest they read this book!

However, if you want one of the bigger waves, look for the guy who's dominating the set waves. Once you decide who that is, go sit near him (but not too close or on the inside position). What's more, it's best if you don't try to paddle for the first few waves. By applying these few tips, he won't feel like you're trying to get one of "his" waves and will be more apt to share with you. In addition, you should keep an eye out for one of the other set waves too. You never know, there could be one that's equally as good if not better!

The next step is to wait for him to catch a smoking wave and surf it really well so that you have a reason to compliment him. When he paddles back out to the lineup commend him on his maneuvers and outstanding surfing ability (everyone likes to be recognized). No B.S., be sincere! In other words, only compliment him if he's truly impressed you. Next thing you know, he'll be offering you a few of the prime set waves. Most of the time, after I've complimented someone, they start sharing waves with me. By the way, the compliment technique can be used with more than one surfer at a time. Still, this scheme shouldn't be done with any great expectations for it doesn't always work. Even if only a few waves are shared without a hassle, be grateful.

Yet, if you're adamant about getting a good set wave, and chose to stay, and hustle for it, this most likely will cause tension (trust me, I'd know). For your sake, when you do get your first wave, you better surf the best that you can to establish that you're a competent surfer. If you do blow it (fall or surf like a kook), you might not get another opportunity. Obviously, it helps to be an experienced surfer for this to work if and if you're going for the best waves.

On the other hand, if this isn't working for you, move in and surf the smaller waves for a while. If all else fails, try one of the other wave catching techniques. You can always head back up to the point and try it again later too. You never know, there may be a new crowd of guys out at the point. Typically, my preference is to catch waves in all the different surf zones. More often than not, I'll use a variety of methods throughout the lineup during most sessions. I'm into quantity as well as quality. My motto is "anything and everything." Of course, a quantity of quality waves is the ultimate goal!

Keep in mind, compliments never hurt and people may share with you regardless. One of the other benefits to complimenting surfers on their rides is it helps create a more positive vibe in the water. This, in turn, makes for a more pleasant surf environment for everyone (except the *Negative Neds*, but nothing will make them happy). Occasionally, the boys in the lineup aren't going to give you a wave no matter what! Thus, this is why I'm sharing an array of methods with you. This next trick I came up with was from years of surfing at the jetties down in Newport Beach. I call it *The Jetty Game*.

10 - THE JETTY GAME

Playing *The Jetty Game* is a risky maneuver. Thus, being a competent surfer is a prerequisite. Honestly, it's downright dangerous! Therefore, please proceed with caution. This tactic will be done at your own risk. Although this technique can be modified and practiced by intermediate surfers, it's not recommended to do so near a jetty. Basically, it'll teach you how to move a crowd around, partially emptying the lineup (at least temporarily), so that you can get a few good waves.

Here's how to play *The Jetty Game*. First, you'll need to accurately determine where the bigger waves are breaking. Then, find some stationary landmarks accordingly. This information will be utilized to help you know where to be when you get back to the lineup. With this in mind, pay close attention to the timing and pattern of the sets. Next, during a lull, paddle past the pack so you're further out and slightly past the Jetty. Then patiently wait and see what happens! Consequently, sitting deeper than everyone else will lure the majority of the guys out of the take-off zone. At first, one or two guys will follow you (and try to sit deeper). Then gradually the rest of the pack will head over too. Next thing you know, they're all trying to out jockey each other to sit the deepest for the upcoming waves. If you really want to move them up the beach, you can continue hustling along with them. This is a psychological game and is contingent upon the guy's egos to help. It drives them nuts when a girl's in a better position to catch a wave than they are!

Meanwhile, keep an eye on the horizon for the first signs of an approaching set. Before the first waves start breaking, nonchalantly sneak back over to the *original* lineup. More than likely, there'll only be a few surfers who chose to stay. This'll better your odds to catch a good set wave while most of the crowd is still too deep. It's imperative to get one of the first few waves of the set (preferably the second or third) before the pack can scramble back over. The timing is crucial. If you move back to the lineup too soon, the pack will follow you. If you wait too long, you'll be left out of position as well. Worse yet, your strategy could backfire and instead of catching a good wave, you could end up being caught by the set and slammed into the jetty!

Keep a watchful eye out for the sets that swing wide. In order to calculate your positioning, use your previously noted lineup. Once you've decided which wave you want, don't hesitate. Start paddling slightly over towards the bay so that you're not too deep. This will give you the best advantage to catch the wave and make it down the line. The swingers are what you're after. They're the bigger shapelier waves that have a longer ride. Anyhow, once the set arrives the group of surfers will suddenly notice that they're out of position. Immediately, they'll start scrambling back over to the real lineup. However, most likely it'll be too late, and you'll already be racing down the line! As stated, this is a dangerous game and you'll want to avoid the jetty at all cost! It's like playing "Jetty Roulette."

You can continue playing *The Jetty Game* throughout the session. It's surprising how well it works! If there's no jetty, the same strategy can be applied using a reef, or an outcropping of rocks. The most extreme technique I've ever used to be the deepest was when I've stood on a rock (or jetty), and jumped into the waves. It's really difficult (if not impossible), to take-off any deeper than that! I've used a similar method by sitting in a small alcove tucked against a cliff (this one was only used during contests). As a result, more risks equals more waves!

The first time I surfed the North Shore was back in the early eighty's. For years, I dreamt of surfing those big Hawaiian waves. Finally, I was prepared to test out my surfing skills. I'd pack up the kids and head off to Hawaii to visit my brother and his family. For the most part, we'd surf in front of his house at Haleiwa Harbor. On the bigger days, Haleiwa is a very dangerous place to surf. The waves are exceptionally powerful and the rips are extremely strong. Thus, they can easily drag you out to sea. Furthermore, there's a shallow inside section where the waves explode on the reef. Appropriately, it's called the *Toilet Bowl* because of the way it flushes you around. Honestly, when the waves get really big, it's hard to find any place safe to surf on the North Shore! Yet, when the waves are small, Haleiwa is the ideal training grounds for the local keikis (kids), to practice their surfing. Also, it was the perfect time for my brother and me to teach our kids how to surf. Afterward, we'd reward them with a famous Matsumoto shave ice.

When the surf was up, my brother and I would leave the kids with my sister-in-law and head out to get some waves of our own. Being that my brother had lived there for a few years, he had the place dialed-in and took me surfing to all the famous breaks: Pipeline, Sunset, Lani's, Rocky Point, Velzyland, etc. Occasionally, we went on a wave hunt to surf less crowded spots. On one of our wave chasing excursions, we ended up at Turtle Bay. We didn't surf in the bay with the tourists but on the other side of the Hotel where it's much more treacherous. It was somewhat crowded, but nothing compared to the premier surf spots.

At first, we were staying on the inside section, patiently waiting to work our way into the lineup (as is the proper protocol). Unfortunately, it didn't seem to matter where we were positioned, neither one of us caught a single wave in over an hour. Not one! "Da boyz" kept taking all the waves. Ruthlessly, they were blocking us from catching any waves, even the little leftovers. In need of a wave, I decided to come up with a new plan. Due to having plenty of time to study the setup, I kept an eye out for different take-off zones. Since the sun would be setting soon, I wanted to at least catch a couple of waves! Ah ha! There's the spot! It was beyond where the guys were sitting that I'd noticed some bigger sets breaking over a partially exposed reef.

After being totally frustrated, I was willing to risk a serious wipeout, and decided to give it a go! If I could catch one of those waves, and make it from there, I'd be stoked! Determined, I told my brother, "Watch this. Now you're going to find out why they call me *Danger Woman!*" His reply was, "Oh no, what're you going to do? If you make the locals angry, they're going to kick my ass! You'll be heading back home, I can't leave, I live here!" No doubt, I was definitely more reckless in my youth, but not to his detriment. Also, I didn't want to piss off the locals in the process. Hopefully, as long as I didn't drop in on them, I'd be okay. Remember, being a girl isn't an excuse either! Sometimes it's helpful. Sometimes it's not.

Nervously, my brother watched as I paddled past the guys to the other side of the lineup. However, I didn't stop there. Continuing, I paddled over to the waves that I had been studying. Praying my calculations were correct, I sat as far over as I dared. This placed me right on the edge of the reef where it was boiling. There was little room for error. The water was extremely shallow, and the reefs were razor sharp. Another thing, the reefs on the inside (which I'd also studied earlier) acted as a barrier in terms of access to the shore. In other words, you couldn't just paddle straight in or surf to the beach. That being the case, if you did get caught inside, you'd have to paddle back out against the surf, and then find a deep enough channel to paddle back in (which happened to be further down the beach).

While I was waiting for a wave I could hear a few of the guys snickering and making comments (even over the sound of the surf). More than likely they were waiting to see this crazy wahine get pitched over-the-falls, and then dragged across the coral reefs. Ignoring them, I was feeling fairly confident that I could make the waves from there and was ready to go for it. No doubt, it helped that my surfboard was a full seven-six gun (Actually, it was my husbands that I talked him into leaving there with me.) As a result, this gave me the advantage of getting into the waves early. Nonetheless, my first ride scared the crap out of me, given the size and nature of the wave. Somehow, I made it over the ledge and landed the vertical (and very turbulent), airdrop. Instantly, I went into a long drawn-out turn while trying to dodge some big rocks. After making the first critical section, I still had to weave in and out around sections of the reef. Once I flew past the guys, and the wave wasn't so strewn with obstacles, I was able to relax and enjoy the rest of the ride into the bay. At first, I bet they thought I was just lucky. However, I continued to pick off some bombs. Only the biggest waves were makeable, therefore they were the safest ones to ride. This wasn't a problem since I was momentarily alone and had my choice of any wave.

Before long, a couple of the guys paddled over but their boards were too short to make the fast, steep drops. They couldn't get into the waves soon enough, which caused them to wipe out. Even if they did make the drop, their boards didn't have enough rail line to make it around the first suck-out section. Needless to say, they'd get worked a few times, before paddling back over to sit with the pack. After watching me get some more good waves (alone), another guy would paddle over and attempt to catch one from where I was (I never hustled them for a wave). Incidentally, he'd have the same results as his friends, a bad wipe out. Soon enough, he too would paddle back over to the pack.

This strategy helped my brother get some waves too. What I'd do was surf past the crowd, then kick-out so that my brother could take-off and surf the rest of the wave by himself. Sometimes, I'd keep going so we could surf the wave together. Now, we were both getting plenty of waves! The problem was, we were running out of time. It wasn't long before it started getting too dark to see. Because I was way over on the reef, I hadn't noticed that everyone else had already gone in. At that point, I was doing my best to stay calm. Believe me, I wanted to panic! After riding one more wave in the dark, I started floundering around through the maze of reefs, until I finally found a channel to paddle in through.

Fortunately, the Tiki torches on the beach and the ancient Hawaiian spirits helped guide me safely back to shore. There's no doubt in my mind that special angels were (and still are) watching over me. On more occasions than I care to remember, I've escaped death both in *and* out of the surf. Thank God I'm not a cat since my nine lives would've been used up when I was a kid. Occasionally, I still tend to push the limits, scaring myself. I wonder if I'll ever outgrow this?

All in all, I don't expect everyone to go to such extremes to catch waves. Mostly, I was trying to figure out how to compensate for not being as strong as the guys, who were constantly out paddling me. On top of that, the rules weren't always played fairly either. There have even been a few times when I've gotten yelled at (or chased off and threatened), for getting tubed behind some guy. Could you imagine what would've happened if it was the other way around? The guys don't like it when a girl surfs deeper than them or is doing something better (or at least as good). Sometimes, simply paddling aggressively would tend to get the boys in a bit of a tizzy! What can I say? Sometimes, a girl's just got to do, what a girl's got to do!

11 - A GIRLS GOTTA DO, WHAT A GIRLS GOTTA DO

Many women capitalize on their good looks and femininity to manipulate men into getting what they want. If that's the only way a girl can get waves, well then go for it! The rest of us have to depend on our brains, survival skills or wave-catching abilities. When it comes to beautiful women men are so predictable. With that in mind, I figured out how to use this to my advantage. With the variety of methods I've used to get more waves, this one requires the assistance of another girl. Such as, whenever my cute friends are visiting from out of town, I take them surfing at some of the local breaks. Unbeknownst to my friends, I use their good looks to shift the lineup around. As a result, I get more waves! This is darn near foolproof!

Once again, assess the conditions but this time before you paddle out note where the main break is and the uncrowded waves that are breaking off to the side. We'll name this backup break 'Site B'. The waves here won't be as good, but good enough to serve your purpose. Start off by paddling out to the main break with your cute friend. Then paddle around the lineup so the guys get a really good look at her. Next, tell your friend that the crowd is too intense and you can both get more waves if you move down the beach. From there paddle over and surf 'Site B'. For the best results, start catching every wave possible. This makes it appear like there are more waves breaking than there really is. More than likely the boys will be thinking they'd rather surf with a couple of girls than in a crowd full of guys. After a while, the majority of them will come over mostly to surf with the hot looking chick. They just can't help themselves!

Meanwhile, while they're all busy gawking at her, sneak back to the main break. This is achieved by catching the smaller inside waves. Now, with half the guys down the beach, the main lineup is near empty. This enhances your opportunity to catch some of the better quality waves. Soon enough, your friend will notice you're missing. When she does find you, she'll paddle back over to where you are. Of course, with the guys in tow! Remain surfing the main break long enough for no one to suspect your antics. Then suggest to your friend to head back over to 'Site B' where it's not as crowded. You can repeat this process as many times as you can get away with.

If you don't have a cute friend with you, this technique of sitting off to the side alone, and catching an abundance of waves still works, but not as well. Now the guys are probably figuring, "If a girl can catch all those waves, then so can I." For that reason, I've done this for years. My friends used to tell me that when they got out of the water they'd enjoy sitting on the beach watching me shift the crowd back and forth from one peak to another! This definitely works best at a beach break where the waves are breaking all over the place. I've also been accused of suckering guys into huge surf. I told them if they weren't comfortable being out there, then why'd they follow me? They never replied. If I were to have to guess, I'd say it was their damn egos again.

There was one time when my girlfriends and I were surfing down at Cardiff Reef in San Diego. It was a super crowded day and hard to catch a wave alone. One of our friends we were surfing with kept dropping in on one guy after another. She was a good surfer and could've easily caught waves on her own, even with the crowd. After seeing her do this several times, we asked her why she kept taking off in front of the guys. She said, *"The boys don't mind because they can look at my butt."*

This was not the answer we expected and it made us all start laughing. After that, we spent the rest of the day taking off in front of each other, especially her (usually with a guy behind her). Then we'd turn around stick out our butts and imitate her, "Want to look at my butt?" It was all in fun, and I must admit that when my friend kept dropping in on the guys, none of them seemed to complain! Cute butt or not, I don't suggest dropping in on anyone. If you're really having a hard time catching waves just ask for one. You'll be surprised at how many guys are willing to give you a wave or share one with you. Occasionally, you don't even have to ask and they'll offer you one. Besides, the boys will have plenty of time to check out your butt, on the paddle back out.

Because my daughter and I frequently surf together, we are totally in tune with each other's styles and idiosyncrasies. Thus, it's not uncommon for us to ride a wave together. Usually, she'll be perched on the nose of her board while I'm smacking the lip right behind her. This forces me to surf vertical, dangerously close to her, but over time she has learned to trust me. Since she was a little girl I told her to just focus on her surfing, and don't look back! We like splitting the peak too. Since she's a regular footer and I'm a goofy footer, most of the time she'll go right and I'll go left. When it's possible, we'll paddle away from the pack and surf the less desirable waves down the beach so that we can be by ourselves. All in all, it's much more relaxing when you don't have to fight a crowd to catch a wave. Yet, more times than not, some clueless dude will paddle over and attempt to start taking waves from us. I've always wondered if it's because we are girls?

Well, this motivated us to come up with a new strategy we call the 'Ham (for Hamrock) Sandwich'. If the guy is being cool it's no big deal, we'll share waves with him. However, if the dude is hustling us, and trying to hog the waves, well then that's a different story. One of us would simply look at the other with a devious grin and say, 'Ham Sandwich?' If the other one replies, 'Ham Sandwich,' the game is on! What we'll do is sit on both sides of him so he's stuck between us. This way, regardless of which direction he attempts to go, one of us will be behind him to call him off. Our usual tactic is to both take-off simultaneously, then fade towards each other sandwiching the guy in. Sometimes, we'd even bump the rails of our boards before turning and surfing in opposite directions. This makes it impossible for the guy to take-off and forces him to pull out. He has now experienced the 'Ham Sandwich.' This is about the same time he realizes that paddling over to where we're surfing wasn't such a good idea after all. Perplexed, he finds it's more difficult to get a wave from two girls than an entire crowd of guys! Consequently, we're then left alone to surf together by ourselves again. To our delight, not once has a guy stuck around for more than a few waves.

For the most part, I've no problem sharing waves with others and splitting the peak. I used to ask guys which direction they were going on a wave so I could surf the opposite way. Too often they'd ignore me, or purposely go whichever way it took to keep me off of the wave. Then I discovered if I simply told them which way to go, and claimed the way I wanted to go, most of the time they'd just do it.

As you know, from the previous stories I've been sharing, being a woman surfer has its own unique challenges. There are both advantages and disadvantages. I've talked to other women surfers (or women from other male dominated sports or workplace) who grew up in the same era. Most of us agree about how intimidating or uninviting it was. The surfing world at that time was still in the beginning stages of accepting women surfers into the lineup. As beautiful as the art of surfing is, unfortunately, there's also the ugly side of surfing.

12 - THE UGLY SIDE OF SURFING

Allegedly, surfing represents freedom. Likewise, true surfers portray a carefree lifestyle that others can only dream of. Surfing is the center of their lives, which leaves almost everything else secondary. Their whole existence will be designed around seeking out the best waves and being free to surf them on any given day. Due to this, surfers have been stereotyped as being noncommittal (except to surf), irresponsible, and unreliable. Of course, that's only a matter of perspective and fortunately an outdated way of viewing surfing (I think). In my generation, our parents used to actually believe we'd outgrow it! Another thing you'll find is that most surfers are avid travelers, often leaving familiar shores to seek unexplored waves around the world. Life becomes the search for the perfect wave. This is because so few things in life compare to the feeling of riding waves. It's so amazing to be in the heart of the powerful forces of nature, especially when you get tubed in big surf! Surfing tests one's ability both physically and mentally. Really, when it comes right down to it, I enjoy the waves whether they are big or small, stormy or calm, good or bad. Of course, every different condition has its own challenges. Just the same, surfing is surfing. For me, it's therapeutic for the soul and inspires creativity. This is probably why so many surfers are also artists and musicians too.

Yet, on the contrary, there's also the ugly side of surfing. This is the aspect of surfing that's not so *Zen*. Due to overcrowded conditions, surfers tend to be territorial, selfish and greedy. Although this has diminished somewhat from how bad it used to be, it definitely still exists. Along with that, there's also the bullying and harassment. The crowded conditions are what contributed to the '*My beach, my wave*' mentality. After years of harassment, my attitude became worse and worse. Unintentionally, I became a bully too. The only difference was, I only bullied the bullies!

Eventually, the day came when I had enough of all the arguing and fighting over waves. As stated, it was long overdue to make some positive changes and get back to pure surfing. In other words, surfing just for the sake of surfing. This was essential for my wellbeing (and everyone else's). Occasionally, I still have a few frustrating moments when it's overcrowded. This tends to happen when I continually get snaked (usually by the same guy)! These are the types of circumstances that tempt me to fall back into my old evil ways!

With this being said, one of the lamest hassles I'd ever been in was when I was surfing at my home break, Huntington Beach Pier. The confrontation happened before I'd even got out to the lineup! As usual, I was paddling out alongside the pier where the current helps pull you out towards the break (it's best to work with the ocean). When I was barely past the first set of pilings this guy started paddling in towards me. He'd paddled all the way in merely to yell at me to get out of the water. At first, I thought maybe he'd mistaken me for someone else, but no one else was around. I couldn't figure out what all the fuss was about? I hadn't even caught a wave yet, let alone finished paddling out. What the hell? He told me to split and threaten me not surf there on my longboard. Then he said, "Why don't you go to Bolsa Chica where you belong!" Bolsa Chica is basically a beginner wave that's surfed mostly on longboards. Anyhow, I thought this guy was on his way in, but instead, he turned around and followed me back out to the lineup. Not only that, he was nagging at me the whole way! At that point, I thought I'd try to just ignore him. The problem was if I stopped paddling, he'd stop. Then he'd sit next to me and continue his grumbling. When I tried to get away, he'd follow me again.

Finally, I said, "Dude, what are you doing? Get away! Why don't you just surf and leave me alone?" I'm not including all the derogatory comments and cuss words he was flagrantly spewing. Eventually, I started using my own share of foul language. Being over this bully, I yelled, "Enough! Shut up and quit your whining! I'll surf wherever I want, whenever I want, on whatever I want, *however, I want.*" Of course, this pissed him off more. Not that I really cared. Next thing I know the other guys in the lineup started harassing me too! Their big grievance was that I was surfing there on a longboard. In response to their comments I said, "Interesting how you guys are cool to me when there's no one else around, but now that you're in a group you start acting all macho with your stupid gang mentality. I can catch plenty of waves on my short board too! The problem is when I do ride my short board here you guys snake me. When I ride my longboard, you all whine like little girls. Huh? Let's see. What board do you think I should ride?" Additionally, I said, "Do you guys have any idea how many waves I *do* share? Do you want me to show you how many I can *really* catch?" In unison, they all said, "Nooo!"

The main bully (I'll call him *Loud Mouth*), said if I caught a wave he'd snake me so I might as well just leave now. My reply was, "Go ahead, what *ever* dude!" Since I couldn't get away from him I decided to sit where I would've as if he wasn't there. *Loud Mouth* kept attempting to intimidate me. In the meantime, he was so busy complaining he didn't notice the wave that was coming towards us. Regardless of the distraction, my focus was on the surf. Therefore, I was in a good position to catch it, while *Loud Mouth*, being on the shoulder, was in a good position to burn me. Determined to make the wave, I dropped in, did a quick bottom turn, and flew up the face of the wave just as he was dropping in. The pointed nose of his board hit me in the shoulder, so I quickly grabbed it with both hands and dragged him through the next bottom turn. Still holding on, I assisted him back up to the top of the wave and then conveniently flung him off of his board. Purposely, I kept a tight grip on the nose of his board and continued surfing, while dragging him behind me. This helped me stall, keeping me in the pit of the wave so that I got tubed. When I thought the wave was going to shut down I let go of his board so I could make the next section. After riding the wave all the way to the pier, I kicked out with a big hoot of taunting laughter. Since it echoed loudly off the underside of the pier, there's no doubt he'd heard it (and everyone else too)!

If *Loud Mouth* was pissed before, he was irate now. He'd been totally humiliated in front of all his buddies. Then, to make matters worse, I started laughing at him. This is when he got in my face and started yelling at me. "You think that was funny?" Still laughing I said, "Yeah, it was. It was really funny." That's when he threatened to rape me in the … Now, I did *not* find that very funny. Before he knew it, I'd shoved my board into his face, stopping at the very last moment. After holding it there for a couple seconds I pulled it back. He probably thought that was it, but I wasn't done. After pulling my board away, I thought about what he said and then threw a punch at him. Again, I held back at the last second, holding my fist about a quarter inch from his eye. Now he knew how easily I could've taken him out! Seriously, it took all my self-control not to hit him. Really, I don't want to hurt anyone, but with that kind of comment, he deserved to be slapped! After that, I just stared him straight in the eye holding his gaze. Without blinking, I gave him a psychotic grin and whispered through my gritted teeth, "Honey, it probably wouldn't even reach. Try taking off on me again and see what'll happen next time." He still continued his whining and complaining, although in a much more subdued manner. Nonetheless, I was furious. How dare he threaten a woman like that! Unacceptable.

One of my team members from the Huntington Beach Longboard Crew (he was about 6'3" 250 pounds) was right there, so I asked him if he'd tell this guy to back off and leave me alone. He said he didn't want to get involved and paddled away. Wow, I thought he was my friend? Since that didn't work, I asked the local high school surf coach for help. He was out there coaching his students (some of whom had joined in on the hassling) and was well aware of what was going on. His reaction was as bad as my friends! He just gave me stink eye and paddled away too. What's wrong with these guys? What a bunch of wimps.

When *Loud Mouth* saw that no one would protect me, he started laughing and getting cocky again. That's when I became reckless and downright dangerous. I started shadowing him around so I could take any wave he went for. It didn't take long to make him back off again. This was done by catching waves and aiming my board straight at him with no intention of slowing down or stopping! I was totally willing to sacrifice my body and my surfboard. I would've happily rammed right into him without a second thought. He knew it too. He made a few more half-hearted attempts to burn me but they were weak. Repeatedly, I'd frustrate him by making sure he couldn't hop me or catch a wave. This pissed him off more than ever but now I was on a mission and there wasn't much he could do about it.

Later, when this other girl paddled out, I warned her that he'd threatened to rape me. This was said right in front of him and now he'd totally lost it. He started screaming at me and calling me a dyke. My response (while laughing), was "Dude, make up your mind, do you want me or not?" This made me laugh even harder! Finally, I told this guy I would've gotten out of the water a long time ago if I wasn't having so much fun hogging all of '*his*' waves. After grabbing a few more waves I split. I was so over it. This whole incident was pathetic.

When I went into the beach I saw a local lifeguard I knew from surfing there with him and his wife. After explaining to him what had happened, he asked if I knew who the guy was, but I didn't. He wanted to know if I remembered what kind of board he was riding or if I happened to notice any of the logos? How about the brand of wetsuit he was wearing? I said no. He told me if I could identify the guy he'd have a talk with him. A couple of days later, I did find out who *Loud Mouth* was (he was a fish vendor for some of the local restaurants). That same day I told the lifeguard, but he didn't do anything. He said I must've provoked it and he wasn't going to bother with it now. That was disappointing I thought his job was to help keep people safe? I'm guessing that *Loud Mouth* must've been one of his bros.

When I'd told my husband what had happened he said, "That's what you get for surfing at the pier." So much for sympathy, whether I can protect myself or not! At least, some of my friends wanted to kick this guy's ass. Thanks, Dave. Honestly, they begged me to tell them who *Loud Mouth* was. I appreciated their concern and I must admit, it was mighty tempting!

After a couple of weeks of coaxing from family and friends, I finally went to the main lifeguard headquarters to file a formal complaint. Knowing the nosey secretary would read the report before passing it on to the chief lifeguard, I didn't hold back with the details. After reviewing the complaint, the Chief called me into his office. He wasn't very happy that this incident took place on his beach. Further, the Chief reprimanded me for not reporting it to him immediately. Apparently, what the guy had done was an assault. He said next time he'd have the guy arrested and thrown into jail. Before I left his office he insisted that for the next few weeks I surf close to the pier. This was so that he could keep an eye on me. Now that's the response I expect from a lifeguard! It's due to altercations like this that there are now laws to protect you. No one has the right to hassle you when you're surfing (or any other time for that matter). Keep in mind though most surf breaks aren't policed like they are in Huntington.

After that, I made a vow to never get into any more fights over waves again. As the saying goes, 'Never say never'. Regrettably, there were a few more hassles. Starting with the one the following week! When I was surfing near the pier (as suggested), some boogie boarder kept dropping in on me. Also, he'd kept kicking water in my face with his swim fins. Wondering what's up, I started getting upset. What's with this guy? Then one of my friends told me it was *Loud Mouths* brother. Oh, that explains it! This new info gave me the green light to misbehave and ruthlessly torment *Boogie Boy*. Beaming from ear to ear, I started dropping in on him. From there, I'd cut back towards him and stuff him into the whitewater. This would force him to be too deep to make the wave. Next, I started turning my board just right so that the spray coming off of the fins would hit him right in the eyes. He'd get so pissed when I'd do that. Therefore, I kept doing it! The hell with my vow, I'll start next week! Humoring myself, I continued making *Boogie Boy* pay for his, and his stupid brothers, rude conduct. I'm happy to say I've never seen either one of them since.

It took one more nasty altercation before I was really done dealing with this kind of crap. This next squabble occurred a few months later down at Blackies (Newport Pier). The break there's what I call the *Old Man's* of North Orange County. Old Man's is one of the breaks at San Onofre. It's known for being a slow mushy wave that even old men (or old women for that matter) can ride. Blackies is a beginner spot that usually has small gentle rolling waves. However, when the Northwest swells hit in the winter, it can get really good with some fairly beefy waves. It was during one of these winter swells when the final skirmish went down.

I was surfing there in the middle of the day during a low tide that was getting lower. Typically, Blackies will get smaller and closed out on a low tide. However, on this magic day, there was enough swell in the water to hold the size even with the dropping tide. Also, the Santa Ana winds were blowing and holding the faces of the waves up, creating some beautiful barrels. Although most of the waves were closing out, there were a handful of really good ones. In spite of that, you still had to kick out before the curtain slammed shut. Since I was surfing alone, I had the luxury of being selective. Thus, I was picking off only the best of the best waves. Also, I was being choosy because I wasn't wearing a leash and if I'd lost my board I'd have to swim in to retrieve it (not that it's a far swim). It's merely another challenge to surf an entire session without losing your board, especially when the surfs rough.

Down by the pier, I noticed a couple of people paddling out. After catching a few waves there, one of them started paddling over towards where I was sitting. He probably saw me get some good rides and figured the waves were better. Admittedly, they were much better! My lineup was straight out from Blackies Bar, which is located about half way between the pier and the jetty at Twenty-eighth Street. The waves by the jetty were the best, but it was too crowded up there. After waiting for a while I saw this killer set wave coming directly towards me. This is one of those rare moments when I'd barely have to paddle to catch it. A one-stroke take-off is another challenge to see how well you can position yourself to catch a wave.

At any rate, the guy who was paddling up from the pier saw this wave too and started paddling as fast as he could. The way this set up was the guy could've easily gone right. I was at the peak and could've gone either way, but he kept paddling towards me. All of a sudden, I realized he might go left. No way! Was this guy really going to paddled all the way up here and snag a wave that was coming straight to me? What's more, because this wave had a nice peak it could've at least been shared. By the way, this is another form of snaking someone. This prompt me to ask in disbelief, "You're not going left are you?" He yells at me, "Yeah, I am going left!" I'm thinking, wow, that sucks. This was definitely an un-cool move, especially from a grown man who looked to be in his sixties.

As if that wasn't enough, this guy (*Old Man* from now on), paddled back out, sat smack next to me with a glare on his face, and then tried to snake me *again*! This time, *I* was going left! During the take-off he imitated me by saying, "You're not going left are you?" So I imitated him back by yelling, "Yeah, I'm going left!" When I paddled back out, *Old Man* was ranting all kinds of things at me. One of his comments was, "Oh, so you think you're more of a man than me?" "Probably," I replied laughing (for some reason laughing seems to piss people off). This caused *Old Man* to mumble some more rude comments. At this point, I looked at him and said, "What is your problem? I was out here surfing all alone when you paddled over here and start hustling me for waves? Look up the beach. See how much better the waves are? Why don't you go over there and surf with the *real* men? See what'll happen when you try hustling them for waves!" Of course, he didn't leave.

Again, when the next wave came in he tried to paddle around me, but this time I was ready and out positioned him. As I returned to the lineup *Old Man* was screaming, "Oh, so you want to have a paddle-battle do you?" He started paddling around me, I mean literally circling around me like a shark! He went around three times while I sat there and laughed at him. I said, "What *ever* dude! You can paddle around me all day if you want. Are you tired yet?" When I said this he quit. What a fool, he had to have felt really stupid. I couldn't believe this guy. Now I've seen it all!

Granted, I'd been out there long enough to have the lineup dialed-in. I knew exactly where to sit when the bigger waves came in. Not to mention, having the advantage of being on a longboard enabled me to out maneuver him for the best ones. Accordingly, this left him stuck with my leftovers. Whenever he did catch a wave and got a decent ride, I'd pretend to be looking the other way like I didn't see it. Yet, whenever he wiped out, which was on most of the waves, I'd be looking right at him with a smile so that'd he know I saw him fall. This was a little psychological game I was playing merely to mess with him. Unbeknown to him, I was also suckering him into the closeouts by acting like I wanted them. This upset him even more because once he was out of position, or had gone over the falls, I'd catch the next wave. No wonder he kept wiping out! To make matters worse (at least for him), I was having one of those magical days when you're surfing flawlessly.

All of a sudden one of the bigger waves of the day came in! I started to charge it but then pulled out at the last moment since it looked like it was going to close out. This got *Old Man* teasing me some more. He said, "Oh, were you scared to take-off? Did that little wave scare you? Chicken!" This guy obviously had no idea who I was or the size of waves I'm capable of riding. As a matter of fact, I'd recently returned from another trip down to Puerto Escondido, which has some of the heaviest breaking waves in the world. This was baby surf in comparison, even at it's biggest! I just smiled to myself since it wasn't even worth commenting on. The next wave was not only bigger it had excellent shape too. Stoked! This wave was breaking further out than all the proceeding waves that day, which in turn forced me to scramble out to meet it.

This guy probably thought I was scratching out to get over the wave and he was going to get it. However, after paddling three-quarters of the way up the face of the wave, I spun around for a steep drop. As I was getting to my feet *Old Man* splashed a handful of water right into my eyes. Luckily, I had experience surfing big waves in hard offshore winds and was used to dropping in by feel alone. In spite of it all, I made the drop and rode the wave, getting tubed like I'd planned on. At the end of the ride, I kicked out cleanly by surfing up and over the back of the wave.

Of course, I wasn't very happy about him throwing water in my face and was trying to decide how I wanted to retaliate. This harassment had gone far enough! His behavior was intolerable! He'd pushed me beyond my limits and I was pissed! Sad to say, but I was thinking that none of this would've happened if I were a guy. Ah, got it! That gave me an idea. Dude, you're screwed!

As I approached him I started apologizing with a compassionate tone of voice saying, "Oh my, I am so sorry, now I understand what's going on here." He stared at me with this perplexed look on his face. After hesitating, I said it again, "Really, I apologize. I know what the real issue is." He's still looking at me trying to figure out what the hell I was talking about when I said, "You must have the small penis syndrome?" This comment caused tears to start welling up in his eyes. He immediately started paddling in without even catching a wave. His response wasn't what I expected.

No doubt, I wanted to piss him off but I didn't mean to humiliate him to the point of tears. It must've really hit a cord. Wow, I almost felt sorry for him. Regardless of what a jerk he was being I kind of felt like a louse. It was bad enough that no matter how hard he tried to get waves from me I kept out jockeying him (and out surfing him), but then I insulted him with a cheap shot on top of it. This made me realize how stupid the whole thing was and I decided that from that point forward, *no matter what the circumstances*, I was done quarreling. Seriously, I didn't ever want to make anyone feel that way again. Remember, how someone treats you is their problem, and how you react is yours (unfortunately, I tend to overreact).

In all honesty, I was hesitant to add these last couple of stories because they're so gnarly. Yet, they were the changing factors that helped me transform from how I used to behave, thus getting the moniker *Danger Woman*, to how I approach things now. Keep in mind these aren't stories from the seventies (when this was common) but from the early two thousands! It was those last few altercations that encouraged me to make some necessary changes in my own behavior.

Temporarily, the pendulum had swung the other way causing me to go from one extreme to the other. In other words, I started paddling away at the slightest sign of trouble and would seek out a new lineup. If they followed me, and I couldn't get away, I'd simply leave. After paddling in I'd sit on the beach and wait until my buddies were done surfing. First, they were surprised because I was usually the last one out of the water. Second, they'd noticed how non-confrontational I was being and asked me if I was feeling okay. They didn't know I'd made a pact with myself (I wasn't sharing it with anyone either in case I couldn't live up to it). No more hassles for sure this time! Ha ha! Maybe someday, never again.

You can thank those 'bullies' for teaching me to mellow out. For after those incidents I can honestly say I've been in very few hassles (if any). Consequently, I'm continually working on acknowledging and improving my lesser qualities, while enhancing my strengths. With practice, it's become easier. Accordingly, I like to feel good about every situation I walk (or paddle), away from. I've found that sharing waves with others is a lot more fun than fighting over them. In fact, I couldn't wholeheartedly complete this book until I'd learned how to walk the walk, not just talk the talk. Trust me, it's been a process.

13 - WALKING THE WALK

A few years ago, my friends invited me to stay with them at their home in El Salvador. Their property is bordered by a river on the North end and includes an entire point of land. As a result, the river mouth combined with the contour underwater, and the way the land juts out, creates a world-class wave. This is a firing right-hand point that breaks over semi-exposed rocks. The house is located at the top of the point and so close to the surf that it's barely above the high tide line! Yet, it's perfect for checking out the waves all day long. That being the case, I took advantage of this by surfing at least a couple of sessions a day.

For a month straight I surfed my butt off! The main downfall was that the point is situated in a way where it's highly visible from several locations. Here's the basic layout of the town in proportion to the point (their property). When you step outside of the gate and head south across the rocky beach, there's an open area under the coconut trees.

This is where the locals like to party and hang out while they're watching the surf. After that, the boardwalk begins. Unfortunately, the last time I was there they were planning to extend the boardwalk all the way up the point right through their land. Hell, right through their house! Anyhow, next is the colorful cemetery. Then there are a bunch of little kiosks (mostly for selling alcohol). Finally, you arrive at the lower part of the town that's built along the bay. It's strewn with vendors, small shops, hotels, and restaurants. Further down the beach, there's a pier. Rumor has it, that on really big swells the waves break all the way through from the point to the pier! Above this area is the main part of the town with the market, more restaurants, a hardware store, pharmacies, etc. Bordering the streets in front of the shops are the stalls with fresh fruits and vegetables.

Also, above the town, there are more houses that are built on the hills overlooking the bay and the point. This is why the surf can be seen from the entire area. It's definitely not a secret spot! Yet, this also served us because when we were in town having lunch, we could see the point too! We'd make sure we'd sit where we could watch the waves. Whenever we'd noticed that the surf was starting to build, we'd quickly finish our meals (or pack it up to go) and rush home to surf. What's more, we would skip our usual routine of shopping after lunch and save the siesta for later too. Surf first, everything else later!

As was our habit, we rode bikes into town but it was really sketchy (bad brakes didn't help). Granted, we had to perform some crazy antics to dodge the buses, trucks, cars, bikes, kids, dogs, an occasional pig, etc.! Jon was a lunatic on his bike! Eileen and I didn't even try to keep up with him. One advantage to having the bikes was it enabled us to get back to the house and be surfing in no time!

Within the first few days of being there I noticed that whenever the waves started to get good the local kids would paddle out. Also, I noticed that this coincided with when the tides were at their optimum. The waves there are very sensitive to the tidal changes. Thus, this can significantly enhance the quality of the surf, or ruin it, depending on the tide. Once I got the tides dialed in, I'd paddle out when the surf was still crappy knowing that shortly it'd start getting good. By doing this I was able to get a few waves alone before everyone else paddled out. This was only possible due to being literally seconds from the surf. Two minutes max if I was lagging!

Whether I was playing guitar, painting, or kicking back in the hammock sipping my favorite coconut *beverage*, I was always ready to paddle out in a heartbeat. I'd stop whatever I was doing and race out there. Since I was already in my bathing suit all I had to do was grab my board, wax it and go! Ah, I love the hot climate and warm water in the tropics! It's so awesome not to have to put a wetsuit on! Anyhow, after grabbing my board I'd skip across the stepping-stones and unlock the gate.

Once I put the key away and was through the gate, I had to slow down to make my way nimbly over the deadly rocks and into the surf. I say nimbly because this was one of the more intimidating rock dances I've ever had to deal with! These rocks aren't only sharp, but they're super slippery, filled with sea urchins, chunks of cement blocks (with rebar sticking out of it), and who knows what else. All kinds of stuff washes out from the river. Your feet could easily slip between the rocks where there are also eels lurking! Worse yet, when the surf was up during the high tide your leg could also get stuck between the rocks! This was because it was both too shallow to duck dive and too big to jump over! There were a few times I thought the shore break was going to break my leg. I chose to pull my leg out and take my chances of getting tumbled over the rocks and scraped up instead (which happened a few times). Not only did I have to scramble over the rocks to get out, but the lineup was strewn with deadly rocks and a couple of giant boulders! One was aptly named Mama Roca. You'd have to constantly be maneuvering around the rocks while you were surfing. This played a major factor in where you positioned yourself for the take-off too. However, this was all worth it for the excellent quality of waves.

At first, when the local surfers paddled out, I'd keep to myself and try to avoid them. When they were in the cove, I'd surf further up at the point. When they came up to the point, I'd paddle (or surf) back down into the cove. My goal was to avoid everyone and the rocks too! Being passive, I never hustled the locals and let them have any wave they wanted. Yet, if after a while they didn't share any waves with me I'd paddle way up the point past all of them. From there I'd take-off super deep over the rocks and boils like I did at Turtle Bay. Hopefully, by taking huge risks like that I'd earn some respect. Either that or they'd just think I was some crazy gringa! That'd probably depend on if I wiped out (or not) and got thrown onto the rocks!

Thankfully, I only had one bad wipe out (besides the shore pound) that dragged me through the rocks. After barely making it through the maze of rocks, my next concern was keeping my bathing suit on (the top came untied and the bottoms were around my ankles). After holding my breath for an extended period of time, I finally resurfaced with my bathing suit back in place. Miraculously, I was uninjured. Actually, I wanted to come up for a breath much sooner (bathing suit on or not), but there was a crowd of El Salvadorian tourists standing right there on the shore watching us surf.

Occasionally, I'd have to call one of the locals off of a wave simply for my safety. This was done in Spanish. From observing their actions and listening to their words I figured out what to say at the appropriate time. Once they saw me ripping up a few of the biggest waves, it was shown that I was an experienced surfer. Also, this is when they realized that I could've easily been jockeying them for waves the whole session if I'd wanted to. I'd catch a few good waves then go back down into the cove to surf the smaller ones alone. Now, they understood that I'd been respecting them by staying out of their way yet, they also knew I wanted a few waves too. If they forgot and started hogging the waves, I'd just paddle past them and sit super deep to remind them. They preferred to leave me alone in the cove. Soon enough we were all sharing waves and having fun surfing together.

After about a week, they started calling up to the house for me to come surf with them (if I wasn't already in the water that is). They even started giving me a few of the better set waves! This made all the waves I passed up when I first arrived worth the sacrifice for, in the long run, I got a lot more waves! In addition, I had made some new friends.

By working my way in with the locals, mutual respect was established creating good vibes in the water. The camaraderie I had established with the kids didn't go unnoticed by my hosts either, for they invited me back to El Salvador the following Thanksgiving. When we arrived the next year, the kids saw me out in the surf and paddled out with big smiles on their faces welcoming me back. This was proof that I was finally "walking the walk." Now, I feel good about living up to the higher standards I'd set for myself by behaving in the surf.

Of course, when I got back to the States I got tested on my patience in crowded surf once again! At least I stayed calm this time! This next incident took place while I was surfing with my daughter in Seal Beach. We intentionally surfed a couple of peaks down from the main break at the pier to avoid the crowd. She was surfing on her usual vintage longboard from the 60's (heavy, single fin). My board of choice (at least at first) was my three-ten belly board (mostly I stand up surf it). Although there were a lot of surfers out (mostly longboarders), I kept seeing some empty set waves roll through next to the pier. Since the surf was better there, I figured what the hell, let's see if I can catch just one of those set waves. It was definitely a long shot, but maybe I'd get lucky.

Amazingly enough, in a short amount of time, I picked off a good set wave. Unfortunately, this guy on a ten-foot log looked right at me and dropped in anyhow, almost on top of me! This forced me to stall to avoid getting hit by his board or running into him. Somehow, I was able to do a few squiggles, and pump a couple of quick turns, to regain the speed needed to stay with the wave. Then all of a sudden he falls right in front of me. Splat! After avoiding a collision and zipping past him, I completed the rest of the ride uninterrupted. When I paddled back out I didn't say a word. Usually, I don't say anything unless someone hops me at least a few times, or they do something really blatant and dangerous. This guy caught quite a few waves and I noticed that I wasn't the only one he was dropping in on. This is one example why I don't take things personally anymore!

Unbelievably, I was able to catch another set wave! Damned if the same *Yahoo* didn't drop in on me again! About half way through the ride he looked back to see if he had stuffed me, but I was right on his tail. Then he turned back around and instead of kicking out, he walked to the nose of his board. In my head, I was thinking, 'nose riding on a ten-foot log, big deal. Dude, am I supposed to be impressed?' Imitating him, I took one step to the nose of my board (that's all you can do on a three-ten) and rode behind him until he fell again. Somehow, I managed to stay on the nose while narrowly missing him. I hung five all the way to the beach to rub it in. What's with this guy anyhow?

This was so lame, I was done struggling on that little board just to be continually burned. This seemed like a good time to change equipment and get on a board that's easier to ride. My rhino chaser should do the trick! Grinning, I put the belly board away and pulled my ten-foot Hawaiian gun out of the back of the van. With the bigger board, it'll be much easier to keep this guy from dropping in on me (or so I thought). When I paddled back out I sat between the pilings under the pier. This made it very difficult for *Yahoo* to take-off deeper than me. He didn't even attempt to! No doubt, it's very dangerous to take-off under the pier. Not only do you have to dodge the pilings, while narrowly missing the seawall, there's also a lot of turbulence.

Being that I was on my bigger board I was able to catch plenty of set waves as well as the in-betweeners. There were a handful of short boarders out so I made sure they got their fair share of waves too. Clearly, I know what it's like to be on a small board when out amongst a group of longboarders. I'd pretty much let them have any wave they wanted. If they caught the wave in front of me I'd kick out so they could ride it alone. Or, I wouldn't even take-off, unless it was to prevent *Yahoo* from going.

Easily enough I picked off another good set wave. Yet, once again the same *Yahoo* dropped in on me for the third time! Not only that, he wouldn't kick out of the wave. Sure enough, he ended his ride like the previous two, by falling. The difference was this time he almost landed right on top of me while his board flew dangerously close to my head. To keep from getting hurt I grabbed his board but it ended up making me fall too. As quick as possible I tossed his board aside and dove out of the way. Luckily my board stayed close by, while his washed into shore. Consequently, we were only in about waist deep water. When the guy finally came up, (I don't know what took him so long), he started yelling at me for being on his wave again. In disbelief, I grabbed my board, got on it, and started paddling away. With a big smile on my face, I said, "That's interesting, I've never been yelled at before by someone who keeps hopping me."

After he swam in to retrieve his board he came back out to the lineup and started yelling at me some more. This is ridiculous! I just smiled and didn't say a word. He kept up his nagging until he pissed off the other surfers. In return, they started harassing him. They'd been watching the whole thing. This was so lame that I asked everyone to let it go and just surf. Next thing you know they're all having a shouting match and I'm the one trying to calm everyone down. The yelling and derogatory comments had escalated to the point to where they were ready to throw some blows. This caused the crowd on the pier to gather and lean over the railing to see if there was going to be a fight.

The boys were still arguing telling this guy things like, "Don't you know who she is? She surfs bigger waves than you ever will! We've never seen your picture in the magazines or seen you on T.V."! I was saying, "Hey, none of that matters, come on let's just surf." The *Yahoo* says, "Yeah, what does that matter?" Then he looks at me and says, "You can't just paddle out here and think you can take any wave you want! You have to work your way into the lineup!" This made the rest of us burst out laughing because this guy looked to be in his mid-twenties (maybe). This is one of those moments when I just couldn't help myself with a smart-ass comment. Smiling, I replied by saying, "Dude, I did that thirty years ago! In fact, I've surfed here since before you were even in your daddy's little nut sack." This really got the boys laughing. They said they've been surfing there that long too and who did he think he was? Then I apologized to the *Yahoo* by stating it must be humiliating to have a chick surfing behind him while he kept falling. He was probably upset too because he saw me sharing waves with everyone else except him. Duh, I wonder why?

Next thing you know someone yells, "Hey Kim, keep it cool they're here to get you." Looking around I'm wondering who "they" are when one of the guys pointed to the lifeguard boat and a Navy gunner boat (I think that's what it was). Now I started laughing again because I thought they were joking, but they were serious. Apparently, there's a very low tolerance here for fights in the water and they actually send in the patrols. Amazing. I've never seen anything like that before, not even in Huntington! It's definitely not the seventies now where you were on your own if there were any altercations! Everyone mellowed out and pretended there was nothing going on.

After a few moments of silence, *Yahoo* whines, "Why don't you just give me a break?" So with a big smile, I say, "Sure dude, any wave you want." He immediately catches a little crappy wave and goes in. It's a good thing too because my friend Sluggo saw what was happening and was on his way out. He wasn't very happy about this guy who kept burning me and then being stupid enough to be razzing me too. Big mistake. Trust me, you don't want to piss Sluggo off! He could be very intimidating weighing close to three hundred pounds while wearing his tight-fitting Speedos (no wetsuit)! He is the mellowest dude in the world unless someone's being stupid like that guy was.

A month or so later I heard through the grapevine that one of *Yahoo's* friends was complaining about how out of line I was the last time I'd surfed there. This is how rumors start! The best part is that he said it to one of my friends who'd happened to be on the beach filming that day. My friend laughed and told this guy he had the story all wrong.

To prove it, he grabbed his video camera out of his van and showed the guy the footage of *Yahoo* hopping me three times in a row. With this being said, it goes to show that no matter what I do the name *Danger Woman* is here to stay! My reputation may take years to change, or it may never change, but that's beside the point, at least I've changed! Well sort of. I still occasionally tend to be a bit of a wave hog.

14 - WAVE HOGS

In retrospect, it was dealing with the wave hogs that taught me how to come up with my own devious wave catching tactics. I wanted to catch as many waves as they did! By the time I got good enough to be a wave hog, I'd also adopted an attitude of entitlement. Once I'd chosen not to have any more confrontations, I had to come up with a new perspective to catching waves (without hogging them or snaking anyone).

The best practice I had was when I spent three months in Costa Rica stand up surfing on a 4'4" belly board. Granted, I had to constantly work on being satisfied with riding a fraction of the waves that I was used to. My board was way too short to out maneuver anyone! Honestly, it took a lot of patience and self-control. It didn't help that I ended up staying in a tiny flat that was located directly in front of the main surf break. This is where the best (and the most aggro) surfers surfed. Due to this, I was constantly being hustled for waves and taken advantage of. Not to mention, that they'd kept burning me even if they'd just caught a wave (or two). In other words, I was dealing with a whole lineup of wave hogs! They were having a field day with me on that little board (probably payback for my own wave hogging Karma).

Instead of getting frustrated I thought I'd use this situation to hone in my wave catching skills. Also, I made a game out of seeing if I could make the wave even if someone was surfing in front of me. I got fairly good at it too! Admittedly, it was fun to see them look back after they thought they'd stuffed me. That was usually right before I went flying past them. That little board was so fast! One day I'd borrowed a longboard and caught a ton of waves, but I still preferred the challenge of the belly board. One good ride on it was better than ten on a longboard!

Years ago, just for kicks, I'd go out surfing on my short board first, find out who the wave hogs were, then go grab my longboard. After that, I'd paddle back out and start hogging all their waves. This was to show them what it felt like when someone wouldn't let you have any waves. For the most part, I prefer to surf alone (there's no one to complain about how many waves I catch)! Likewise, it's why I'm constantly moving around in the lineup and often surfing at different beaches. I like to mix it up. Besides, this is my way of not wearing out my welcome. In addition, I'm not the type to sit around and wait for a wave to come to me either. Overall, I get a rhythm going by keeping in motion. To tell the truth, if someone were to watch me surf they'd see that I caught a tremendous amount of waves (without hogging them). Yet, if they're observant they'd also notice that ninety percent of the waves I rode were crap, the ones that no one else wanted. Whether it appears like it or not, I don't catch nearly as many waves that I'm capable of except when I'm surfing alone.

One summer, up in Oregon, I was giving a surf lesson at a place which is known for having ruthless locals. I wasn't too concerned because I knew that it was more in the winter that the locals fiercely guarded their waves. Although we were in the cove, where the waves (and the surfers) aren't as intimidating, we still didn't want to be in the way or piss anyone off. Therefore, we surfed further down the beach away from everyone else. This was to be respectful of the surfers in the lineup. Also, it's dangerous (and not cool) to teach beginners how to surf in crowded areas, or where there are experienced surfers.

Regardless, during the surfing lesson, some guy paddled out of the crowd over to where we were and started hogging the waves. To make matters worse, not only was he on a longboard; he was also dropping in on my student! Because I was on a short board there wasn't much I could do about it except use it as a learning tool for my student as what *not* to do! When I could, I'd take-off deeper and call the guy off so that my student could catch a wave. This instruction was prearranged with the student so he knew that when I yelled at the wave hog, he could go. The guy couldn't complain about being burned either because at the same time he was burning me.

When the surf lesson was finished I paddled over to the main lineup to catch a few waves before going in. Who do you think started paddling around me, hogging the waves again? Yep. Same dude. All I wanted were a few waves after the lesson. This is why I decided to paddle all the way in, grab my longboard, and paddle all the way back out. It was a big ordeal considering the length of the paddle, the scramble over the rocks, and the freezing cold water. Believe me, the cold water alone shortens the surf sessions considerably. This was an indication of how pissed I was because I can't stand cold water! No doubt, I wasn't very happy to go through all this, but I was determined to teach that guy a lesson while catching a few waves at the same time.

Let me tell you, that guy didn't get another wave for the rest of his session. Except once, when out of sheer indignation he hopped me. Luckily, I had enough speed to go up and over the lip of the wave right past him. Then with all that speed, I did a gouging cutback coming back directly towards him. He probably thought I was going to surf right into him but at the last moment, I quickly changed direction to continue my ride. Too late! I'd already stuffed him into the white water and made him fall off of his board. After that, I didn't give him another opportunity to take-off in front of me. If he attempted to, I'd haul ass and aim my board directly at him (sound familiar)!

Several waves later, after I outmaneuvered him again, he blurted out, "You must be catching all the waves because you're smaller and lighter!" His remark wasn't worthy of a response. If believing that made him feel better then, whatever. Shortly thereafter, he paddled in. That guy was the worst kind of wave hog there is, a kook hog. He was the type of guy that rode a long board to simply to compensate for his lack of wave catching skills.

Later, when I got out of the water and was climbing into my van to change (and get warm), this old-time surfer walked up to me and told me how he had witnessed the whole scene. Even though he was snickering about it and found it humorous, I was kind of embarrassed for retaliating instead of letting it go.

Every day there's an abundance of epic waves that go by unridden. In fact, if you sat on the beach and watched the waves on a really crowded day, you'd still see some good empty waves go by. All in all, by learning to think in terms of abundance, it'll be easier for you to share waves with others. I'm constantly reminding myself that there'll always be more. Too bad it took me thirty-some years before I finally figured this one out! Further, with so many surfers riding longboards, and now SUPS (which are both easier to catch waves on than short boards), it's even more important to share waves. Because I ride both short and longboards, I've been on both sides of the stick! This is why I suggest, if you're a good surfer and can easily out position others, giving up a few waves to stoke them out.

On another note, I must warn you that there are some beaches where you may not be welcomed regardless of how kind you are or how well you behave. These are the surf spots where the local surfers have a bad attitude. Locals Only! Please, pay close attention to the following chapter. Dealing with local surfers is an art in itself, and believe me, it's best to be respectful, or else… When it comes right down to it, it's all about respect. Having respect is the only chance you have of *maybe* being accepted into the lineup. Remember, when you are surfing at others home break you don't want to shit in their neighborhood. In other words, you're just a visitor with a day pass, if you're lucky.

15 - LOCALS ONLY

SURFING LOCALIZED BREAKS

When you find yourself surfing at a break that's known (or maybe not known, but will quickly be found out), to be heavily localized, it's wise to work your way into the lineup slowly. Better yet, it'd be in your best interest to surf elsewhere. These are the breaks where outsiders are clearly not welcomed. Yet, if you do choose to paddle out at *their break* (meaning the locals surf spot), the best advice I can give you is: DO NOT PADDLE STRAIGHT INTO THE LINEUP AND START TAKING WAVES! This would be disrespectful. It's best to start off by observing the waves and locals for a bit. Then, depending on the situation, ride some of the smaller inside waves or the leftovers that others have missed or don't want. Warning; don't attempt to paddle for the same wave as one of the locals. More than likely, this would piss them off causing them to band together and gang up on you. Also, they'd make it damn near impossible for you to catch any more waves. More than likely, there'd be a good chance this action would get you escorted back to the beach, or worse yet beat up! And for God's sake, by all means, don't drop in on any of them (unintentionally or not)! By taking your time and working yourself into the lineup slowly, you'll have a much better chance of getting some waves. Believe me, the mellower you are, the better.

At some places, it's best if you don't try engaging them in conversation or even making eye contact. Just keep to yourself. Shredding on your first few waves helps too. You can be sure they'll be watching. If your surfing abilities are less than par, or if you paddle out clueless of the social structure, more than likely you will be preyed upon like an injured animal. Every location is different and you'll have to feel out the crowd and figure it out for yourself. No doubt, I've had plenty of experience in this area.

There have been many times when I've surfed remote places in the world with only a few locals out. Whenever possible, I would surf off to the side or down the beach a ways. This shows the locals that I am respecting them. Gradually, I'd paddle (or surf) over to where they were. From there I'd sit and watch them catch waves hoping they would invite me to surf with them. If not, I would catch a few on my own and see how they reacted. If they were super aggro I'd simply paddle back down the beach to surf the lesser quality waves. On the other hand, if they were cool I'd be patient and only catch a few waves. Most importantly, you don't want them to feel threatened that you're going to take one of their waves. If you handle yourself properly they may let you have a few waves.

A good example of working your way into the lineup properly was when I was staying in a quaint little surfing community that was hidden in the jungles of Brazil. As usual, I took a walk down to the beach to check out the surf (and the surroundings). The waves weren't very good straight out in front of the hotel, so I kept on walking. About a mile down the beach, I noticed a little sand bar breaking with perfect two to four-foot waves. There was a soft offshore breeze blowing. To my delight, there were only about a half dozen locals out. Being that I'd already checked out the waves from one end of the cove to the other, I decided this was the best place to surf.

It was fairly late in the afternoon so I ran up to the road (noting some landmarks so I knew how to get back), and hitchhiked back to the hotel. After I grabbed my board and left the hotel key at the front desk, I hitched a ride back down the road.

Once I got dropped off (at the previously chosen landmarks), I ran across the beach and paddled out. I started off about fifty yards away from where the locals were surfing. Of course, the waves weren't half as good or big there, but they were good enough. No worries, I had a strategy. With the sun quickly dropping, I caught as many waves as I could in the shortest amount of time possible. Then, I surfed to the best of my ability to catch their attention. The offshore winds had picked up a bit. This created some really fun hollow barrels. Needless to say, I got shacked several times. Gradually, I moved closer and closer to the lineup. Yet, I was cautious and made sure to stay out of the local's way. I didn't want to take any wave they might want.

Before long, they invited me to surf with them. They even started giving me waves merely to watch me surf. We started taking turns making sure everyone got waves. This created a really fun surfing environment.

The sun was already down so I figured it was time to head back to the hotel before it got any darker. Besides, by then the offshore winds had really started howling! I've got to tell you, carrying a longboard in strong winds is no easy task! It was quite a chore. Saying goodbye to my new friends, I trudged across the beach back to the road hoping for a ride. Ironically enough, the same woman who'd picked me up earlier ended up picking me up again. Thank God she gave me a ride back to the hotel and I wasn't stuck in the dark with a long walk. She happened to pick me up quite a few times during my visit and we both laughed every time.

By the way, the locals and I had so much fun surfing together we ended up hanging out for the entire trip. They told me about some hidden surf breaks in the area, but none of us had a car so we only surfed in that little cove. At least they clued me in on the best tides to surf and the idiosyncrasies of those breaks. Also, they shared the best places to eat and where the jungle rave parties were happening. Nothing like local knowledge!

The next morning, when I was on a mission to get some red nail polish (superstitiously, I didn't want to compete without it), one of the local girls I'd surfed with offered to help me out. She said she knew a place that would have it for sure. I sure hoped she was right because I had already checked every shop in town. When we started off there were a couple of guys (Americans) that wanted to tag along. We went so far into the jungle they started to get sketched out. They thought she might be setting us up to get jumped. Both of these guys were big and knew martial arts yet, they were still uncomfortable.

Finally, we came around a bend in the road and there was this tiny little shack. They sold a variety of objects, including the sought after red nail polish. After buying the polish she took us further into the jungle instead of back towards the beach. Now the guys were really getting scared. I told them to head back if they weren't comfortable. I didn't ask them to go in the first place! Anyhow, she ended up taking us to her house so she could paint my nails. That's when I realized that she was trying to make some money. Grateful for her hospitality I paid her to paint my toenails and my fingernails! She wanted to make some extra money by giving the guys massages too! They didn't go for it, at least not then. Finally, we headed back to the beach where I gave her a surf lesson.

There was another time when I went surfing at a heavily localized break up in Northern California (a place I'll keep unmentioned). This time I was allowed to surf with the boys without getting vibed for a unique reason. By the way, if you do happen to come upon a good surf break that has locals only, don't tell anyone else about it! *If* you're invited back it's best to go alone, or *maybe* with one friend, but definitely no more than that. And no cameras either! Taking photos at some places could mean a death sentence (at least a broken camera)! Anyhow, my friend Ann, her dog Molli, my oldest daughter, Nina, and I went for a hike. We wanted to check out the surf during the sunset. After we made it down the muddy path through the forest of eucalyptus trees, we came to the top of a bluff. Looking out over the cliff we were greeted with the sight of pumping surf. The waves were glassy with a solid six-foot swell exploding over the shallow reefs. Unbelievable! Earlier in the day, the waves were almost completely flat and it was blown out.

My God, is there time to run back to the car, drive down the hill and get my board and wetsuit and head back to surf before dark? I had to at least try! Why does it always seem like I come upon surf like this right before dark? When I go surfing I prefer to surf for several hours at a time. Oh well, some waves are better than none! After leaving my beautiful sixteen-year-old daughter on the beach with the dog (for protection), and all the good-looking boys, Ann and I raced back to the house for my surf gear.

Fortunately, my friend knows and understands me well and was more than willing to help. She drove back to the house like a maniac, negotiating the curvy mountainous road. When we got to her house I grabbed my board and wetsuit and threw the board into the back of the truck, taking the wetsuit up front with me. She drove even faster back up the hill while I struggled into my thick wetsuit. This was no easy task, but by the time we arrived I was dressed and ready to go. We ran back down the slippery trail. Rapidly waxing my board, I took another quick survey of the treacherous surf that was breaking over the now semi-exposed reefs. I've surfed there before so I wasn't totally unfamiliar with the lineup, yet it wasn't like I had it dialed-in either.

After taking a big breath to relax, I jumped off the rock shelf into the freezing cold water and paddled like hell. Although I was letting the rip help pull me out, I was also struggling to make sure it didn't drag me down the beach in the opposite direction. The currents there are very strong. It was a long paddle out around the reef to where the guys were sitting. I wanted to catch the big set waves that were breaking beyond where they were, but I knew if I paddled straight past them it would piss them off. There wasn't much time before it got dark so I had to time things just right. On this occasion, I thought it'd work out best if I sat with the locals first. Even though I started catching a few of the smaller, more insignificant waves, I still kept an eye on the bigger sets breaking at the far end of the reef.

For some reason, the guys were being uncharacteristically friendly. Normally, the guys there won't even talk to me? After a few rides, the boys asked if that was my daughter up on the beach. I confirmed that she was. Oh, now I get it! This is why they were being so friendly. Nina must've left quite an impression on them! They started telling me how cool they thought she was. Apparently, she'd had told them about my national titles and my *Danger Woman* nickname too. They were even letting me have a few of the better waves! The guys were also intrigued because I'd paddled out alone into such gnarly surf on a longboard. I must admit it was intimidating. Also, it was more challenging on a longboard because of the quick directional changes required to exit the wave (especially backside). Most of the waves had long ridable walls but then at the end, they'd close out and slam on the reef. It must've been a really low tide.

With the sun already down it was well into the feeding hour, particularly in these sharky waters! It was time to make my move. After the next set, I paddled past the boys to the deeper section of the reef and caught the waves I'd come out there for! These were the gems. Instead of the locals getting angry because I was taking off past them (which usually pisses them off), they were stoked to see me scratch into a few thick bombs. This was apparent from their hooting and hollering.

In fact, this got everyone all jacked-up to surf harder and push the limits (my specialty). Subsequently, we enjoyed the last few waves of the day together until it started getting too dark to see. There was still the trek back up the hill to the truck.

CAUTION: THERE ARE NO GUARANTEES. PADDLE OUT AT HEAVILY LOCALIZED BEACHES AT YOUR OWN RISK.

Now don't get me wrong or let me paint a rosy picture where you think that by just being a girl, being kind, or even following the sacred laws of surfing, you can work your way into any lineup. Some of the more gnarly spots are off limits and the locals won't ever accept an outsider, period. Once my friends and I had a gun pulled on us. The guy fired off a few shots into the air as he was screaming at us to split! Another time, the local natives insisted we pay a compensation for surfing the waves on their reef (in some parts of the world each village owns the reef, the fishing rights and the waves in front of their homes). Additionally, at some surf spots, you could literally be chased off, or have rocks thrown at you before you even paddle out. If you do happen to make it out as far as the surf, there's a good possibility you'll return to a vandalized car with all your gear ripped off. It's not nearly as common as it used to be, but it's still going on out there so be informed. Further, you have to keep in mind that at most places there won't be anyone to enforce the rules or protect you either.

For the most part, I think I've just always been lucky. On one of my Hawaiian Island surf trips, I was surfing on the West Side of Oahu at Makaha. It's an intimidating surf spot if you're not from there. The waves are scary enough when it's big, add the locals and it's even less welcoming. That's how most of the West Side surf breaks are. This is the Hawaiians turf. Very local. They'd much prefer that the tourist stayed in Waikiki. I don't blame them. This is their playground. At any rate, one time when I was surfing there I ran over the second biggest guy in the water. Believe me, that was one really big boy! Of course, it was an accident. Seriously, I was scared to death of what the consequences might be. Here's how it happened.

There was a perfect eight-foot wave (Hawaiian style) that came thundering in and shifted slightly over towards the bay. This was where I was paddling back out after the previous ride. There was a guy paddling out that was a ways ahead of me. When he saw the unridden wave he spun his board around and snagged it at the last moment. I was thinking, Damn! *That wave looks so good. If only that one guy wasn't there, I could've had it!* Before I'd finished my thought, the guy kicked out for no apparent reason. Sweet, I can't believe my luck! There was barely enough time for me to spin my board around and catch this primo wave! This is the type of wave you dream of getting to yourself, especially at a crowded break like this. All day long you're telling yourself, *if I could get just one good set wave, alone, I would be satisfied.* With all this going through my head, I didn't realize that someone else (the second biggest guy in the water), was paddling out right behind me with the same idea in mind, *Am I really going to get this wave alone?*

Anyhow, when I whipped my board around for a quick one-stroke take-off, the wave lurched up faster than I expected. As a result, after barely getting to my feet, I ended up bouncing right up and over this big guy. This caused me to run directly across him, body and board! *Oh Shit!* I heard the crack of my fins hitting his board and the softer sound of my fins hitting his body. Somehow, I stayed on my board. Selfishly, I chose to keep surfing. Oh my God, look at this wave! It had about a twelve-foot face, it was totally lined up, and I was alone on it with no one even attempting to catch it! The entire ride I kept asking myself if I should kick out and go see if he was okay? After getting some air off of the backwash, I continued riding the wave further down the beach until it ended in the sand.

Now what do I do? Should I paddle back out and check on him? Should I just run to the car and drive off! Nope, can't do that. Besides, I'd driven to the West Side with four other women and I couldn't leave them there. What started out to be a beautiful dream wave turned out to be quite stressful. I knew better. I should've kicked out immediately and made sure he wasn't hurt! That would've been the right thing to do. Instead, I'd chosen to keep going. Eventually, I decided I had to accept the consequences. Therefore, I paddled all the way back out to check on him.

Oh man! Now I was really stressing. Is he going to pound me? If he hit me it'd probably kill me! He outweighed me by at least two hundred pounds! The guy was easy enough to find in the lineup. I approached him very cautiously as I paddled up to him (but not too close). No doubt, I wanted to make sure that I'd kept a safe enough distance between us in case I had to paddle for my life. I started apologizing and asked if he was okay. *"Wat da matta with you sista? You not see me or wat?"* (I mean, come on, how could I miss him?) Apologizing again I tried to explain to him that the wave had done something really funky, and bounced me right on top of him. Seriously, I hadn't meant to run him over, it was a freak accident. Luckily, he agreed. One last time, I asked him if I'd hurt him, knowing I'd heard the sick thud of board hitting flesh. He said, "No, but you ding my board sista, and I jus fix it yestaday." I told him I was sorry and I'd give him some money to get it fixed. He seemed surprised. "Really, sista?" "Of course," I said. That was the least I can do. At that point, I was ecstatic just to be alive! He said that twenty dollars would cover the cost. Hell, the wave alone was worth twenty bucks! Next, I casually looked at my watch and told him I was going to surf for about another hour. Then I asked him to point out which car was his so I could put the money through the window. In good faith I described the rental car to him in case he got out before me and needed to find me.

When I got back to the car I told my friends what happened. They laughed at me. Then they asked if I was really going to pay him. Looking at them with disapproval I said, "Of course I am! I'm crazy, not stupid." In all honesty, my goal was to pay him before he came looking for me, so he'd know I wasn't going to bail on him. Well, it didn't quite work out that way. On the contrary, of all things, I was strapping my board onto the racks of the car. This is when he pulled up in his truck asking for his money. I'm sure it appeared as though I was leaving. Without hesitating I grabbed the money and happily paid him. That was the best twenty dollars I'd ever spent! I'm glad I made the right choice (well kind of, I should've kicked out and checked on him immediately).

When my friends and I got back to the North Shore, we ran into a photographer we knew. He suggested that we go to Makaha the next day for a photo shoot. If I hadn't faced my problem (fear) head on, I wouldn't have been able to go back there. Not only for the photo shoot but ever! The thing is, if you ever hurt someone (or possibly hurt someone) it can be a matter of life or death depending on the severity of the injury and how fast you respond. Looking out for your brothers and sisters in the water is always the right thing to do. I'd never left an injured surfer in the water before or since that incident. What was I thinking? Oh yeah, I was scared (fear will cause you to make poor choices). OK, I'll admit it. The wave was really good too!

The next day, during the photo shoot, I saw one of the Hawaiian girls that I'd given waves to while we were competing on the North Shore. She was stoked to see me and showed her aloha by giving me a few good waves. The second biggest guy in the water, the one I'd run over the day before, was also being super cool to me. He greeted me with a big grin on his face and showed me where he'd already fixed the ding on his board. Likewise, he gave me a couple of good waves too! Some of the other locals were probably wondering, "Who dat haole chick?" To this day, I can surf Makaha with a good feeling and the Aloha spirit. Also, I ended up getting a full page spread in a magazine from the photo shoot that day. In the photo, I was getting some air on my eight-foot gun off of the infamous Makaha backwash.

Although surfing can be tarnished at times by some of the behavior (territorialism and bullying), that goes on out in the water, there are still plenty of places to surf where you won't have to deal with that. Albeit, most likely, it won't be at the premier surf spots. Especially the point breaks! Yet, by being educated on what's really going on you'll have a much better chance of survival. Hopefully, these tips will help you work yourself safely into any lineup.

On another note, by observing all the different levels of surfers, their styles, techniques, and behavior, it'll help you improve your surfing skills tremendously. Watch and learn. This is how I learned what, and what not, to do and catch more waves. Nevertheless, regardless of having over forty years of surfing experience, I'm still learning. This just goes to show you, it's never too late to teach an old dog, new tricks!

16 - NEVER TOO LATE TO TEACH AN OLD DOG NEW TRICKS

Believe it or not, you can teach an old dog, new tricks! When I was younger I used to be terrified of getting old simply because I thought when I was in my fifties I'd be too old to surf. Yet, at fifty some years old my surfing is still progressing. As I got older and older, my attitude about age changed. Hell, I rode the biggest waves of my life in my forties, and I'm still charging. Best yet, after surfing with Jon, my seventy-nine-year-old surfing buddy, I felt really young! He rips! Not only does he rip he does it on a short board. I'm not talking about a fat, thick, old man short board either. His boards are lightweight high-performance surfboards that range in size from five-ten to six-two. In addition, he rides them in double overhead surf over deadly rocks! Jon is so energetic I like to joke around and call him the oldest kid I know!

Of course, he's not the first elderly man (or woman) I've surfed with. Over the years I've surfed with a handful of surfers in their eighties, but they were on big oversized longboards in gentle rolling surf.

When Jon and I spent a month surfing together in El Salvador, I asked him if he'd coach me. In return he said he would, but only if I'd coach him. With this agreement, we started helping each other out and as a result, we both progressed respectively. Primarily, this was because we were both open to learning and improving our skills. The only thing I felt Jon needed to work on was taking a few extra strokes on the take-off. This helped him be further down the face of the wave, which in turn allowed him to get his bum knee underneath him easier. Other than that, he was already taking off deeper than most of the guys in the lineup, as well as going faster. Damn, if he wasn't hitting the lip harder too! Amazing. In return, he helped me with my backside form by encouraging me to surf more vertical and with more rotation. He did this by teaching me how to use the weight of my arms more efficiently for more power in my turns. Without a doubt, he's inspired me mostly by showing me that it's still possible to short board and rip, for at least another thirty years (I hope).

It seems that when I was a kook and first learning how to surf, I was given a rough time. Then when I got good, I got hassled for ripping. It must be pretty tough for some guys when a girl can out surf them. This used to make me feel awkward, but what was I supposed to do? Surf bad so they'd feel better? Now I realize it's their own issues they've got to deal with, not mine. It doesn't help that I tend to catch more waves in one session than most people do in a combo of sessions.

There have been many times when people have approached me after I've come in from surfing simply to tell me that they're exhausted from just watching me surf. Laughing, I'd merely smile. To this day, the sheer thrill of gliding across the water makes me happy. I love the feeling of turning as hard as I can. If I see a wave that only allows me to fit in one solid move, I go for it. This is what I call the "One

Maneuver Merry." Sometimes that one move can make my day! Whether the waves are one foot and sloppy at Blackies (Newport Pier), or perfect twenty footers at Waimea Bay, I enjoy it all! As always, I just want to surf and have a good time.

There's no doubt I enjoy living life to the fullest. This is why I strive to surf to the best of my ability and am constantly pushing the limits. The better you surf the more fun it is! I've worked very hard to get where I'm at through sheer willpower, perseverance, and clocking thousands of hours of water time (paddling and surfing)! In addition, I create goals for myself and then set out to accomplish them. Consequently, these same principles are applied to all areas of my life, not just surfing. I'm not afraid to take a good honest objective look at myself. This means the good, the bad, and the ugly! It starts with self-awareness, and then with that comes responsibility. Not everyone wants to accept his or her faults or less desirable traits. In fact, I've noticed that it's not uncommon for people to feel threatened when someone's doing something better than they are. From all appearances, they'd prefer to tear another person down rather than work on improving themselves and living up to their own potential. I've even noticed that some people get pissed off if you're happy! How sad.

Well, it may be too late to teach some old dogs new tricks, but not this dog! I intend to surf until the day I die, or die surfing, whatever comes first!

Original Artwork by DW
Kim Hamrock

Killer Dana 8 1/2 x 11 Acrylic/Canvas

Fish Dive 16 x 20 Acrylic/Canvas

Hey Joe 10 x 11 Oil/Canvas

Cloudbreak 14 x 18 Oil/Canvas

My Amakua 14 x 18 Oil/Canvas

Margeaux Hamrock   Photo: Brian Asher

Mustard, Margeaux & Kim   Photo: Brian Asher

Chris Hamrock   Photo: Ray Zimmerman MRZ Photos

Danger Woman – Newport Beach, CA   Photo: Elizabeth Pepin

Sunset Beach, HI

Kim Hamrock – Mid-seventies skate sessions

Surf School In Oregon

Danger Woman – Waimea Bay, HI

Danger Woman – Puerto Escondido, MX   Photo: Ruben Pina

Danger Woman – Newport Beach, CA   Photo: Tom Cozad

Danger Woman – Costa Rica

Danger Woman – Costa Rica   Photo: Scary Barry

Danger Woman – Huntington Beach   Photo: John Lyman

Nina Hamrock   Photo: Tom Chavez

17 - SURFING SAFETY TIPS

There's so much to learn before you even start surfing. The two main things that terrify most beginner surfers, besides sharks, are being hit by a surfboard (usually their own), and surfing in crowds.

Here are a few guidelines and basic safety tips that will help inform you on what, and what not, to do while you're surfing in the lineup. Also, you'll learn about different ocean conditions pertaining to surfing.

KNOW HOW TO SWIM

It seems like knowing how to swim would be a no-brainer, but I've seen way too many people panic when they lose their surfboard. To my astonishment, it was because they didn't know how to swim very well, or not at all! For your safety, not only should you know how to swim, but also you should know how to swim in the surf. Start off by going out with someone who is experienced with the ways of the ocean. They can help show you how to get familiar in working with the waves and currents. You'll find that swimming in the ocean is completely different from swimming in a pool or a lake. Learn how to bodysurf.

STAY CALM

The most important tip, besides knowing how to swim, is to STAY CALM! Learning how to manage your fears to prevent yourself from panicking could save your, or somebody else's life. One way to accomplish this is to train yourself to relax through breath control and meditation.

BE AWARE & PAY ATTENTION

Once you enter the ocean you'll have no idea what type of situation you may find yourself in. Pay constant attention, and be prepared for anything. This includes keeping an eye on the horizon for an approaching set. It's of the utmost importance to be aware of everything going on around you. This includes what's in front, behind, to the side, above, and what may be lurking below. The ocean is extremely unpredictable and does weird things when you least expect it. This demands that you are able to quickly shift from one moment to the next while being completely focused on the now. Please, use common sense. It's all a moment-by-moment process that happens very fast. Being alert will help prepare you for a variety of circumstances, and may also help prevent an accident.

NEVER TURN YOUR BACK ON THE OCEAN

Turning your back on the ocean seems like another no brainer but I've seen some pretty hideous accidents happen to people who weren't paying attention (tourists and surfers). Of course, your back will be to the ocean when you're paddling into a wave (or surfing backside). Even then, you'll want to take one last quick glance over both shoulders as you're stroking into a wave. This is a good habit to form. Be sure to watch the wave while you're riding it too. The bottom-line is to know what's going on around you at all times.

There are numerous reasons why you don't want to turn your back to the ocean. One of them is to make sure a wave isn't about to crash on you. Also, there could be someone surfing a wave right behind you or a loose surfboard bouncing through the soup. Because surfboards are made with foam they're buoyant, yet they are also made of fiberglass, which makes them hard. The thing is, if you don't look you won't know. Another thing, if someone does lose their board in the surf, only retrieve it for them if it's safe to do so. Trying to grab a loose surfboard bouncing in the soup can be risky, even if the waves or white water are really small.

DO NOT THROW YOUR BOARD ASIDE

When it comes to surf etiquette, tossing your board aside is one of the number one no no's. This is a good way to get frowned upon, if not yelled at! Back in the seventies, you would've gotten beaten up and kicked out of the water. Please don't put someone else at risk because you don't want to deal with going under a wave. No ifs ands or buts about it. Hold onto your board!

Wearing a leash is no excuse either! Carelessly tossing your surfboard aside, even with a leash on, your board could still hit someone behind you. Do the math: Suppose you have a nine-foot board, with a nine-foot leash. Nine plus nine is eighteen. Now, include the length of your leg, and the ocean dragging you back. Someone could be over twenty feet behind you and your board could *still* hit them. No joke, I've witnessed loose boards in the surf that have caught a piece of chop and flown ten feet up into the air or shot twenty feet across the water in an instant (now you know why you have to be careful grabbing a loose board). This is no exaggeration! I've also had my leash stretched out to twice its length and half of its diameter when getting dragged in big surf. They do stretch!

There are very few exceptions to this rule and you'd better have a damn good excuse for breaking it. One excuse would be if there's another surfer coming towards you, and there's absolutely no way to avoid being run over by them or hit by their board. Then you can break the cardinal rule of tossing your board aside. But, before you do so make sure that there's no one paddling behind you. If someone is there - DO NOT TOSS YOUR BOARD ASIDE! What you can do is call out a warning so that they have an opportunity to possibly get out of the way. If all else fails, hold on and hope for the best. Occasionally, you can throw your board away from someone before diving under but you better be sure it won't hit them! Use your best judgment with everyone's safety in mind. There have been times when I've held onto my board no matter what due to someone being right behind me. Sometimes I was able to bounce over them, and other times I got slammed right into them, board and all. If you do get thrown into someone no doubt they'll be bummed, but not as much so if you toss your board in front of them.

Another exception is when the waves are huge. I don't mean four to six feet or even eight to ten feet. I mean REALLY BIG! Like a situation where you'd be seriously injured if you even tried to hold onto your board. Most surfers in this type of surf are highly skilled or should be, and have big wave experience. They understand the dangers and are extra cautious of their surroundings as well as being aware of where the other surfers are around them.

The only other excuse for throwing your board aside would be if no one else were out surfing or swimming or even along the shoreline. If you toss your board aside (with a leash on) you are also risking the wave breaking your board or snapping the leash.

With this being said, I'd like to suggest getting in the habit of staying with your board by knowing how to hold on to it (duck-dive, turtle-turn, etc.). Even if you do wear a leash, surf as if you don't have one on, and would have to swim in if you did lose your board. There are a variety of techniques that can be used to keep your board with, or close, to you. By close, an example would be to kick your board out behind the wave before it closes out (do not do this with a leash on). This has to be done just right so you have time to swim to your board and retrieve it before the next wave gets it.

Make kicking out an art form. Have fun and experiment with different techniques of exiting out of the waves. Besides, ending the wave cleanly makes the entire ride feel complete. If you do it right, you can surf over the back of the wave, lie down on your board, and use the momentum to paddle back out, all in one smooth motion. Of course, you can finish your rides by doing one last big maneuver instead of kicking out behind the wave. It all depends on the situation.

NEVER HAVE YOUR BOARD SIDEWAYS BETWEEN YOU AND THE WAVES

One of the first things I teach, and then mention several times throughout a surfing lesson, is: NEVER HAVE YOUR BOARD SIDEWAYS BETWEEN YOU AND THE WAVES! I repeated this so it'll sink in. When it comes to surfing, rarely can you say always or never. This is as close as it gets. Please approach the oncoming waves straight on. Once you're experienced you can deviate from this slightly, but for the most part, it's perpendicular to the oncoming surf. Every wave comes in at a slightly different angle, so you'll need to be constantly readjusting your board according to the angle of the wave. If you have your board at the slightest angle to an oncoming wave it can be either knocked into you or ripped out of your hands. Even a small wave can propel it into you with a tremendous amount of force. It's equally important to have the correct angle when you're paddling into a wave – If you don't, you could either pearl (not enough angle) or miss the wave (too much angle).

DO NOT PADDLE BEHIND ANOTHER SURFER

The danger of paddling out behind another surfer is that if a wave comes it can easily wash them back knocking them into you. This is a good way to get a fin in your forehead. I've had to remind my students on more than one occasion not to paddle out behind me. They think because I'm an expert and know what I'm doing it's okay. It's not okay! The waves will toss me back as easily as anyone. The ocean is completely indifferent and couldn't care less who you are or how much experience you have.

For your safety, keep at least two board lengths distance between you and another surfer when you're paddling out side by side. This way, if the wave does knock you around, there'll be enough space between you to avoid a collision

LOOK BOTH WAYS BEFORE TAKING OFF ON A WAVE

Hopefully, when you were young, your mother taught you to look both ways before crossing the street. Likewise, when you're driving, you'll look both ways before pulling out into traffic. Well, the same goes for surfing! This serves more than one purpose. First and foremost, you'll want to make sure no one else is already on the wave or in the priority position for the take-off. What's more, this will help you see what the wave is doing. By closely observing the wave, and its ever-changing nature, you can position yourself more accurately to catch it. The wave could suddenly jack-up, flatten out, or, it may shift altogether.

WAVE CATCHING TIP

Do your best to build up momentum so that you can match the speed of the swell. You can do this by catching the swell as it's forming into a wave. Be careful not to out paddle the wave and get too far in front of it. Sometimes this can happen when the wave hits a shallow spot and jacks up. In this case, back off paddling until the wave catches up to you, then take a few quick hard strokes to rematch the swell speed again.

On the other hand, if the wave goes into deep water, this will cause it to slow down. Now it will require taking a few extra hard strokes to catch it. Not to mention, waves can also shift to the right or left, forcing you to readjust your position. Remember, the ocean is in control so it's up to you to adjust accordingly. Once you decide you're going for a wave, totally commit and paddle hard! The number of extra paddles that you'll need will vary according to different situations. In big surf, I've taken up to twenty or more extra strokes!

THREE MORE STROKES

This is the general amount of EXTRA STROKES you'll want to take AFTER you think you've caught the wave. Really, 'three more strokes' is simply a reminder to take enough paddles to make sure that you're into the wave. The mistake most beginners make is to stop paddling and stand up too soon. There are a few different things that can happen when you don't take enough paddles.

One: You miss the wave. That's usually the most forgiving option unless there's a big set behind you. Two: You have a late out-of-control drop forcing you to go straight. This will cause you to miss the open-faced part of the wave leaving you stuck in the foam. Three: You totally biff it, and pearl. Four: You get stuck in the lip of the wave and pitched over the falls. Thus, taking a few extra hard strokes before standing up will help you be successful in catching more waves.

FALLING

There is an art to falling properly. Most importantly get away from your board and cover your head! Keep your head covered until you know where your board is and block the board if it's about to hit you. It hurts less when you get hit in the arm than in the head. When you fall try to land in the whitewater if you can. This will put you behind your board. Another thing, when it's shallow land flat! If you fall backward tuck your tailbone in! Sooner or later you're going to pearl (nose-dive). It will be inevitable that you'll fall in front of your board. In this case, just flow with it but don't come up right away. A good rule is to say your name and the word wait before you come up. ALWAYS COME UP WITH ONE HAND FIRST with the other arm covering your head.

DO NOT DIVE OFF OF YOUR BOARD

Don't dive off of your board or from shore into the ocean! The bottom surface is uneven and you could hit a shallow spot with your head and cause a serious spinal injury. This applies to all types of surf breaks. Don't let the sand fool you! The force of the ocean can make a sand bottom feel like cement! If you're forced to dive off your board, dive as shallow as possible. Once again, try to fall away from your board into the whitewater or onto the face of the wave.

Sometimes, when I wipe out, providing that I'm not wearing a leash, I'll dive away from my board into the wave and body surf in. This saves me from having to swim in and helps me get to the board (or beach) quicker. Besides being practical, body surfing is fun and it conserves energy as opposed to swimming in. Do not do this if you're wearing a leash (your board can hit you).

The sooner you can retrieve your board the better. This can help prevent it from hitting someone or breaking on the beach.

RETRIEVING A SURFBOARD FROM THE SHORELINE
To safely pick up a surfboard that has washed ashore, stand sideways so you can see both the ocean and the beach at the same time. If there are no waves simply pick it up. If it's washing around in the surf line wait until it settles down before you grab it. Now, if it's safe to do so, pick it up. If there's a wave right there, and there's not enough time to get your board, then get out of the way! The board can get washed up the beach and hit you in the process. Also, watch out as it gets sucked back down the beach towards the water where it can hit you again. Consequently, I've seen people endanger themselves in the shore-break by simply not paying attention. They think because they're on the shore they can let their guard down. I don't let my guard down until I'm far above the high tide line where the water can't reach me!

During one of my very first surf sessions, I watched my friend bend down to pick his board up off the beach. At that same moment, a little wave bounced his board up into his face and knocked one of his front teeth out. Learning from his mistake, I made sure this never happened to me (or one of my students)! I make it a point to learn not only from my mistakes but others too!

KNOW YOUR LIMITS
Only surf in waves that match your surfing ability. Of course, I encourage you to slowly push yourself beyond your comfort zone a little at a time. This way you can build up your confidence and continue to improve your surfing skills. Yet, be careful not to do this to the detriment or safety of others. Being a beginner you'll want to find a small mushy wave to start on. A slow rolling wave can be identified by

the way the white water crumbles down the face. On the other hand, you'll know the waves are breaking hard when the lip of the wave pitches out and breaks on the flat water at the bottom of the wave. Realize, that the waves can be small and don't have to be pitching to be powerful. Another way to tell how hard it's breaking will be by how high the whitewater explodes when the wave breaks. The higher the whitewater, the harder it's breaking or the shallower it is.

DO NOT SIT INSIDE THE TAKE-OFF ZONE WHERE OTHER SURFERS ARE DROPPING IN

Not only is this hazardous but it can really piss the other surfers off. When an inexperienced surfer paddles out into surf that's beyond their ability they put everyone at risk. Stay out of the more crowded areas and from where the more experienced surfers are surfing. At least until you have control of your board and know how to handle yourself in the lineup. Start off in small gentle rolling waves away from others, preferably with a buddy and where the lifeguards can see you.

ASSESS THE SURF CONDITIONS BEFORE PADDLING OUT

When you first arrive at the beach to go for a surf there are a few things you'll want to pay attention to (I like to utilize this time by stretching). First, you'll want to note the size of the waves and get a feel for the power of the swell. Watch at least a few sets (you may even want to time them). Next, observe which way the ocean or the current is drifting (if at all). Check to see if there are any rip currents (or rip tides). What's the tide doing and how does it affect that particular break? How about the winds? Also, get a feel for the surfers and their abilities. Be sure to look out for any other hazards. Example: piers, jetties, rocks, reefs, marine life, other surfers, etc. Start checking out all the conditions when you arrive and when you're done surfing and you will see how the conditions are constantly changing.

PHYSICAL CONDITIONING

Surfing can be a very strenuous form of exercise. It is highly recommend that you be in top physical shape before taking up surfing. This includes a good stretching program to help with flexibility and to lessen the chance of pulling a muscle. Stretch before and after surfing. Also, regular chiropractic care is a key factor in overall health. One of my secret training tools is the use of the INDO Board for strengthening, stretching and balance.

RIPTIDES, RIP CURRENTS AND UNDERTOWS

First off, an undertow is just a strong rip. Sometimes rips are easy to identify and sometimes they're not. There are a couple of things you can look for. The water where the rip is will be browner than the surrounding water. This is from the turbulence pulling the sand up from the bottom. Another would be little ripples (waves) of water flowing seaward. When it's glassy this is easy to see, but if the surface is slightly ruffled or windy it's not as noticeable. If you can easily identify a rip more than likely it's going to be a strong one.

When you paddle out, you should PADDLE TO THE SIDE OF THE LINEUP away from where everyone is catching waves and surfing. This is usually where the channels are. The channels can have a slight (or strong) flow of water that can help pull you out. Be cautious, this is also where the rips form. Experienced surfers know how to work with these rips to get out to the break faster. I don't suggest doing this until you're familiar with the ways of the ocean and a strong confident paddler.

'Riptides' or 'rip currents' can appear, disappear or shift very quickly. If by some chance you do get stuck in a rip, and cannot get out of it, stay with your surfboard and use it as your flotation device. Even if you are better at swimming than paddling the board will keep you afloat much longer.

Don't fight the rip by trying to paddle straight back towards shore against it. This will only tire you out and use up the energy you may need to get back to the beach. It's best to WORK WITH THE OCEAN not against it! If there's a side current pulling (which you should've noted before paddling out) go in the same direction that the water is flowing. To get out of a rip, paddle parallel to the beach or at a forty-five-degree angle, towards the beach. Get over to where the waves or white water can help take you back to the shore. Before paddling back out, reassess the conditions and make sure you're well rested first. The rips, like the ocean, are unpredictable. They can take you far up the beach, pull you way out to sea, or simply subside. How far or long, who knows?

IF YOU EVER NEED HELP:
WAVE ONE OR BOTH ARMS OVER YOUR HEAD

This is a universally recognized signal for help. Don't panic! Remember, one of the first tips is to always STAY CALM.

WINDS
The winds create the waves, and the winds can deteriorate the waves. Good surf is dependent on the right wind conditions. They can make or break a surf session. Strong winds can be dangerous regardless of which direction they're blowing.

- Onshore Winds: Onshore winds break the faces of the waves down, creating walled waves with lots of choppy sections. Thus, making it difficult to get a good open faced ride. When a wave closes out in front of you, you must know how to straighten out (or kick out), in time. If not, the wave can easily flip your board over and hit you.

- Offshore Winds: Although offshore winds are highly desired by experienced surfers, and excellent for creating tubular waves, they're not very safe for beginners. It's difficult to paddle against the winds to catch a wave, making the timing critical. This is because the offshore winds hold the faces of the waves up until the last moment before the lip pitches out. This causes the wave to have a steep, late drop. Another effect of the offshore winds is that it blows water into your eyes. Not only does it sting, it makes it difficult to see. Besides that, when you fall your board can easily be blown back into you. Another thing you'll have to watch out for is if you're not wearing a leash, your board could blow out to sea faster than you could retrieve it.

-   Side Shore Winds: Side shore winds can be good or bad depending on the strength and angle of the wind. Sometimes it can make one direction of the wave be blown out, while the other direction is hollow.

-   Glassy Conditions: Glassy conditions are when there's no (or very little) wind. Kelp beds can help keep the surface water glassy too. This creates beautiful conditions for surfing. Yet, sometimes when it's super glassy it can make it difficult to differentiate the waves from the sea or horizon. This is quite common when it's overcast. The waves will appear to come out of nowhere making it difficult to see where to position yourself. This also puts you at risk of having a wave (or set), suddenly appear directly in front of you, or worse yet right on top of you! A surfer could not see you too (or vice versa).

LOOSE DEBRIS AND SEA LIFE

Loose Debris and marine life are other hazards to be aware of. There is always the possibility of debris floating in the surf. Coming from Southern California this rarely crossed my mind, except after the occasional big storm. I really became aware of this unexpected danger when I was surfing in Northern Oregon and a big log went over the falls, barely missing my head. This happened when I was in the tube and it was the last thing I expected! If it had hit me it could've easily knocked me unconscious seriously injuring me, or worse yet killed me! From that point forward, I paid closer attention to this hazard and incorporated it into my surfing lessons (even in the more gentle waters in So Cal).

The treacherous waters of the great northwest required being intensely alert. For instance, besides trying to watch the student's surf and trying not to turn my back on the ocean, I also had to keep an eye out for big logs, strong rips, and dangerous sea life. This included crabs that were big enough to remove a toe!

Another surprise was when a river otter came out of nowhere. It popped up right next to me, swam in, and then ran up the beach teasing the dogs. I had no idea they were that big, let alone swam in the ocean, or could run so fast! Oh yeah, I had to watch out for the nasty tempered local, Arthur too! He's a big mean sea lion whose breath alone can scare you out of the water. Arthur didn't appreciate anyone surfing in his fishing grounds at the South end of the cove (my favorite spot). That was his turf and he'd let you know it. We made a deal; as long as I didn't eat his fish I could surf there!

On top of everything else, there are the ever-lurking Great Whites. With up to thirty women in my all-girls surf clinics, you know at least one of them was probably attracting sharks. Girls, if you're on your cycle, and surfing in sharky waters, think twice! It's one thing doing so at your own risk, but you'll potentially be putting others at risk too. This goes for anyone who may have a cut or is bleeding. Plain and simple, blood attracts sharks. Therefore, if you're bleeding, paddle in, even if it's not known for being sharky. This is another factor in being aware.

SURF LEASH, LEASHES

(Leg Rope, Leggie, Cord, Goon Cord, Etc.).

If you choose to wear a surf leash get one that's approximately the same length as the surfboard. This is important for safety reasons. If the leash is too long, you can't retrieve your board quick enough. This could result in the wave getting it before you, and then having it thrown it into you. If it's too short, it can spring back and hit you before you can get away or block it. The leash should be worn on your back foot so that there's less chance of tripping over it. It's best to attach it on the outside of your wetsuit in case you have to detach it quickly. On some beaches, it's mandatory to wear a leash (which I personally don't agree with but understand). Overall, leashes are dangerous, but there are a time and place for them. When it comes right down to it, wearing a leash is a personal preference. Here are some of the pros and cons of wearing a surf leash so that you can decide for yourself if you want to wear one or not.

PROS:
- The board is less likely to hit someone.
- Your surfboard stays with you so you don't have to swim in after a wipeout (unless your leash breaks).
- When surfing at rocky beaches the leash can help protect the board from being damaged. Also, if you lose your board and have to walk over rocks (or reefs), it reduces the risks of getting cuts or injuries to your feet (or knees, ankles, etc.).
- In cold water, you want to have as much of your body out of the water as possible. Swimming in to retrieve your board is enough to bring your body temperature down very quickly. When the water is super cold or you've already been out for a while, this may result in hypothermia.
- When you fall, you can feel the board tugging on your leg so you'll have some idea of where it is.
- If someone is unconscious, others will see the nose of the board bobbing up and down (known as tomb-stoning). This is a good indication that there's someone attached to the board under the water. We've rescued a number of surfers who would've probably drowned if we hadn't seen their board tomb-stoning.

- In strong offshore winds or heavy currents, your board won't be taken out to sea if it gets separated from you.
- If you get stuck in a rip it'll keep your surfboard (your flotation device) attached to you.
- Wearing a leash can help you feel more confident to practice new maneuvers, or get deeper in the tube, knowing you won't have to swim in if you don't make it.

CONS:
- False sense of security - A LEASH IS NOT A LIFE-SAVING DEVICE (except for the tomb-stoners). LEASHES CAN AND DO BREAK!
- Can more readily cause your board to spring back and hit you.
- Could wash in and hit another surfer, swimmer, or someone standing at the water's edge.
- Can wrap around you and seriously injure you (fingers, toes, neck, etc.).
- May also drag you under water for extended periods of time. This makes it difficult to come up and could potentially cause you to DROWN.
- They can get caught on rocks, coral, kelp, the pilings of a pier, or any other underwater obstruction.
- Gets caught in the kelp and can cause you to come to a complete stop and get flung off of your board.
- May get tangled up with another surfer (or surfers leash) if you both wipe out too closely or have a collision.
- Leashes cause undo stress to joints and ligaments, especially knee leashes. The stress is increased with a bigger heavier board, like a standup paddleboard (SUP).
- May get tangled around your feet, or stuck between your toes, and cause you to trip.
- If you step on the leash you can roll right off (like stepping on marbles) or do the splits.

- Often the leash will trip you when you're cross stepping on a longboard. This interferes with getting to the tip of the board for a nose-ride, or when you're back peddling.
- Can hog-tie your feet closely together, causing you to lose control of your board or wipe out.
- Causes drag in small surf slowing you down.

EXTRA LEASH WARNINGS

ONLY SURF IN WAVES THAT YOU CAN COMFORTABLY SWIM IN WITHOUT A BOARD!

Be prepared to swim in if your leash breaks even after a heavy wipeout or if you've just taken a set on the head. In this situation, the best advice I can give is, "WHEN IN DOUBT, DON'T PADDLE OUT!" Seriously, if you don't think you can confidently swim in after losing your board and getting worked, play it safe and don't go out. Find another break or wait to surf on a calmer day. You know your own abilities. Make the correct choice – IT'S YOUR LIFE!

There are several reasons why I'm personally not keen on using a leash. For one, I've had it get stuck in kelp while it was simultaneously wrapped tightly around my neck. I was literally tied to the reef flat on my back and was held down like this in as little as ten inches of water. This was one of those moments where I was forced to stay calm (this is another time I wanted to panic). All I could do was slowly untangle myself from the kelp one strand at a time, then deal with unwrapping the leash from my neck. This was one of the closest times I'd ever come to drowning. I remember thinking if I only had a straw I could reach some air! I think the only reason I didn't drown was because I would've been too embarrassed to in ankle deep water!

I can't tell you how many times my leash has hurt me. I have a saying, 'It never hurts to swim." I've had it wrap around my neck, break my fingers, break my nose, yank my earrings out, hog-tie me from my neck to my knees pinning my arms to my body, etc. There have been times when it's gotten stuck around a rock knocking me around and holding me down uncomfortably long. I've seen other surfers hanging from the pilings of the pier unable to reach up and detach their leashes.

The thing about surfers who don't wear leashes is that they learn to stay with their boards more readily. They know that they'll have to swim in if they do lose their board. Thus, time spent swimming is time not spent surfing! As a result, they don't just carelessly toss their board aside, or jump off at the end of a ride. Likewise, they tend to focus on surfing more precisely and are in tune with their swimming abilities. This means no surprises when you find yourself boardless out in the surf.

TAKING CARE OF YOUR EQUIPMENT

SURFBOARD
Check your surfboard regularly to make sure there are no dings, cracks or buckles. Any one of theses will cause your surfboard to absorb water and compromise the integrity of the board. Not only that, the dings and cracks can give you a nasty fiberglass cut. Also, once a board is buckled it won't be as strong. It can actually break while you're surfing on it, or more likely when you're *turtle turning* under a wave.

Believe it or not most dings on your surfboard will happen when you're not surfing. This can be taking it in and out of your car, room (or wherever you keep it). Airline baggage handlers have ruined many boards. A good suggestion is having the proper type of board bag to protect your stick.

Another thing, don't leave a surfboard in the sun or inside of a hot car. This can cause it to delaminate. This too will weaken your board and make it more prone to breaking.

FINS
First, make sure the fins are put in correctly and properly secured. Also, check for a cracked fin or fin box. If the fin or box is cracked, replace it. A broken fin box can cause the area around the box to take in water. This can weaken it and cause it to break out altogether, losing fin and

all. What's more, sometimes fins are razor sharp and can easily cut you. For this reason, I recommend sanding the tip and back edges lightly to make them duller. You can also sand them if they get nicks on them.

LEASH

It's a good idea to inspect the condition of your leash periodically. Look for any cracks or tears in the urethane as well as making sure the Velcro isn't old and worn out. Another thing, be sure to attach your leash to your board properly so it won't come untied. Start by using a strong piece of nylon cord, not a shoestring, hair tie, or anything else that could easily break. On top of that, if the nylon cord isn't tied properly, leaving it too long, it can cut right through the rail of the board. This was common before the rail saver was invented. If your leash does break, it's best that you throw it away rather than try to fix it. Once it has been compromised it won't be dependable.

Don't' keep your leash wrapped around the tail of your board when you're not using it. This can cause it to tangle around your feet when you're surfing (or when you're sitting on your board).

SURF WAX

They make wax specifically for surfing. Most other waxes are designed to make surfaces slick. Whereas, surf wax is designed to be tacky so you don't slip off of your board. There are different wax formulas for different water temperatures (cold, cool, warm, tropical, etc.). Use the appropriate wax accordingly. There are also different methods to waxing a board. For some, waxing their board before surfing is a ritual. Regardless of how you wax your board what's more important is where you wax it. The proper way to wax your board is to wax the deck (top) and partially on the top part of the rails. Be sure to wax where your hands are placed when you're pushing up to get to your feet too. A poorly waxed board can be dangerous due to slipping off.

Out of habit, I wax my board every time before I surf. What's more, I tuck some wax into my wetsuit (or trunks, it falls out of my bikini) and take it out surfing with me. This is in case my board gets slippery while

I'm out there. Another thing, when you walk over slimy rocks on the way out your feet will get slippery. Then when you start surfing you'll slip off, even with a good wax job. To remedy this I'll wax the top of my feet before I paddle out. Once I've finished walking over the rocks, and start paddling, I'll dip them in the water and then rub the bottom of one foot on top of the other. This waxes my feet. It may seem strange but it works!

How often you remove all the old wax build up, and re-wax your board, is a personal preference. I've known some surfers that believe it's taboo to ever change the wax. I prefer my boards to be lightweight so I change the wax fairly often. As a pro, I wanted the board clean so the sponsor's logos would be highly visible for contests or photo shoots (not that it always was). To each their own.

By the way, if you get sand in the wax of your board it can feel like heavy grit sandpaper. This can tear you up when you're paddling unless you have a wetsuit or a rash-guard on. In the process, it can leave you with a nasty wax rash. Many times, it's hard not to get sand in your wax. It's kind of a catch twenty-two when it comes to resting your board in the sand when it's hot out. If you leave your board deck up the wax will melt off. If you place your board wax down, you'll get sand in it. In this predicament, try to find a rock, a log, or something to keep most of the board out of the sand. If there's nothing to place it on you can use your backpack or a rolled up towel to serve the same purpose. When I didn't have anything at all, I would make a mound of sand and gently rest the nose (or tail) on it leaving most of the board out of the sand. Don't leave it in your car deck up either or you'll have wax drip all over the seats. Store your wax in a container that doesn't leak if the wax melts and try not to leave it the sun or where it's hot.

WETSUITS/RASHGUARDS

Wetsuits are primarily designed to help keep you warm. They're made of neoprene (a synthetic rubber that stretches). They come in different thickness and are measured in millimeters (Example: 5/4, 4/3, 3/2, etc.). The thicker the warmer.

They make everything from vests, to full suits, for different climates and conditions. A wetsuit can prevent hypothermia in really cold water and will prolong your surf sessions. There are also accessories like hoods, booties, and gloves to give you extra warmth. The booties can be used for both keeping your feet warm, and to protect your feet from sharp objects. Additionally, a thin wetsuit or rashguard can be used in warm waters to protect you from the sun, the reef or rocks, or simply to keep you from getting a wax rash.

Choose the appropriate wetsuit depending on the region, or season, you are surfing in. A proper fitting wetsuit is an absolute necessity. They're designed to let just enough water in for your body to heat it up. Therefore, if it's too big the water will constantly be flushing in and out of it and won't keep you warm. Not only that, the wetsuit will fill up with water making it heavier. On the other hand, if it's too tight you'll be restricted and it can tire you out very quickly. It'll also cause a wetsuit rash (different from a wax rash). Most rashes from ill-fitting wetsuits will be under the armpits, from paddling, and in the neck area. If you get any rips or tears in your wetsuit you can repair it with heavy thread (or dental floss), and wetsuit glue. Or better yet, take it to a professional.

If you want your wetsuit to last, rinse it out in fresh water when you're done surfing. Be sure to hang it in the shade, not the sun where it will cause it to deteriorate and ruin it. Also, use a thick hanger or one made specifically for wetsuits to decrease the stress on the material.

RESPECT

Start by respecting each other and your differences (we already covered respecting locals). It's important to also respect the environment. This means doing your part to help keep the beaches and oceans clean. Respect the sea life and marine protected areas. Stay on marked trails so you don't cause erosion. Make it a habit of leaving the beach cleaner than when you arrived. If your board or leash breaks, dispose of them properly. If you see a wild animal that's injured call the local rescue unit. Do your best to protect it from further injury. Or people bothering it. Don't stress it out by approaching it too closely. Lastly, remember, it takes all of us to help preserve our planet and Mother Ocean.

Now that I've covered some basic safety tips and courtesies it is time to learn about SURFING ETIQUETTE. They go hand in hand yet the next two "rules" are the meat of surfing etiquette.

Although all of it's important, these rules (and not tossing your board aside), are the ones every surfer is expected to know and abide by.

18 - SURFING ETIQUETTE

SURFING ETIQUETTE: THE ESTABLISHED CODE OF BEHAVIOR IN A SURFING SOCIETY OR WITHIN A GROUP OF SURFERS

There was a time when there were so few people who surfed that they'd be happy to see another surfer out in the water with them.

Fortunately, there are still a few places like that! Yet, when it became overcrowded with the resurgence of surfing in the late fifties and early sixties, newcomers were no longer welcomed into the lineup. As stated earlier, by the seventies surfers were downright ruthless and discouraged others from surfing through various bullying techniques. Inevitably, the need for some form of order was destined to develop. Therefore, with this integral component of the social aspect of surfing, rules then became necessary for safety reasons.

These rules would not apply if you surfed alone, but more than likely you'll be surfing around other people. Many novice surfers are completely clueless that there's a proper protocol to follow. Understanding, and abiding by, the rules will make it safer for everyone and help you be more comfortable in crowded conditions. Straight up, it's the prerequisite to surfing and should be known before working your way into any lineup. Of course, if you choose not to follow the rules, be prepared to pay the consequences. The first thing you'll need to know is the difference between a right breaking wave and a left breaking wave.

WAVE DIRECTION: RIGHT/LEFT

The wave direction is always determined by the SURFER'S PERSPECTIVE WHILE PADDLING INTO A WAVE TOWARDS SHORE! In other words, if you surf towards the right, it's considered a right-breaking wave, and if you surf to the left it's a left-breaking wave. When you're standing on the beach it will be the opposite (like stage right or stage left). When you hear someone call you off a wave by saying, "Going right" (or left), you better know which direction they're talking about.

For years I couldn't figure out why my kids had such a difficult time learning their right from their left. Later it dawned on me that they grew up on the beach where I was constantly pointing out a great *left* (or *right)*, wave to them. Yet, when they went to school they were taught that right and left were the opposite of what I'd taught them (sorry kids). Inadvertently, I'd taught them from a surfer's perspective. The confusion was most apparent when I started teaching them how to drive. "No! The *other* left!"

THIS IS THE MOST IMPORTANT SURFING ETTIQUETE RULE: **DO NOT DROP IN ON ANOTHER SURFER ALREADY RIDING A WAVE!** THE SURFER CLOSEST TO THE PEAK OR DEEPEST HAS THE RIGHT-OF-WAY

Disregarding this one rule has probably caused more fights in the water than breaking all of the other rules put together (believe me, I'd know)!

When I was on the U.S. Surf Team our coaches taught us to 'Use our neck muscles'. Plainly put, LOOK BOTH WAYS BEFORE YOU GO! Of course, if two surfers are taking off on the same peak, they can share it by going in opposite directions. If you're not sure which direction someone is going, then ask them. At times there'll be a broken section of a wave (this is where the white water's crashing down) between two surfers. In this case, if the surfer who's deeper can't make the wave, then you can go. A word of caution: Better be darn sure they aren't going make the wave or do a floater or an aerial over the broken section. By the same token, watch out for surfers that take-off behind the peak to set up for a tube-ride (this is what I meant about being the deepest).

There have been times when I've been the deepest for the take-off but it's questionable whether I can make the wave. In this instance, if someone else is positioned where they can make it, I'll pull out and let them know that they can go. It's embarrassing to call someone off a wave and then miss it. It's way cooler to let someone else go and wait for another one. Of course, if no one's there I'll go just for fun to see if I could make it! I would rather try, and fail than constantly be thinking of that wave I might have made. I've made some and totally ate crap on others.

PADDLING OUT - THE SURFER RIDING THE WAVE HAS THE RIGHT-OF-WAY

The surfer riding the wave has the right of way, period. Therefore, if you're the one paddling out, it's up to you to move out of the way. Besides, it's common sense so that you don't get run over. Likewise, you'll be expected to PADDLE BEHIND THE SURFER WHERE THE WAVE HAS ALREADY BROKEN. This allows the surfer to continue riding the open face of the wave without you interfering with their ride. The wave may break right on you but that's better than being hit by the wave, a body, and a board! Now, if you can't safely get behind the surfer riding the wave (it all depends on where you are both positioned) then paddle over the shoulder as quickly as possible and get out of the way. Don't hesitate! Once you decide in which direction to paddle, stick to it. By doing this the surfer riding the wave can anticipate where you're going and can avoid you.

Once again, be sure to pay close attention and plan ahead. Do your best to calculate what the wave and surfer are doing so you can determine the best approach. What's more, keep in mind that good surfers are very fast and will be down the line before you know it. Whatever you do, don't just sit there like a deer in the headlights of an oncoming car! Subsequently, if you do just sit there, more than likely you'll get run over. For some reason, it works like a magnet and the two of you always seem to come together much faster than you anticipated. After years of surfing, and teaching, I still can't tell you why this happens, but trust me it does. Although it's rare, sometimes sitting still may be the safest thing to do. Remember, the ocean is in a constant flux and can change very quickly. It's up to you to be ready to flow with the changes.

If you're paddling out and see a surfer ripping up the wave and making quick directional changes, this will indicate that they have control of their board. Of course, this doesn't always mean that they won't accidentally run over you. I've been run over by both experienced and inexperienced surfers. If someone is getting dangerously close, and you still have enough time, do a deep duck dive under the wave to avoid them (on a longboard you can turtle-turn but watch your fingers). If you can't get out of the way and are about to be slammed into, it's better to sacrifice your board than your body. Use your board to block yourself if it'll prevent you from getting hurt or help lessen your injuries.

If you absolutely have to, and ONLY AS A LAST RESORT, toss your board aside and dive under the wave. First, make sure no one is behind you! If there is, hold onto your board and try to get bounced away from them. Sometimes you can use the buoyancy of your board to help you do this. Other times, there's nothing you can do and you'll have nowhere to go. This is a good time to start praying! Don't just presume you'll be seen either.

WHEN IN DOUBT, SHOUT! Sometimes the surfer mistakenly thinks you're hooting for them, but that's okay, at least they will hear you and know you're there. Now, if there's an out-of-control surfer, most likely a beginner, coming straight towards you, and you can't get out of the way, well then you're in trouble and you better *really* start praying!

Don't think because someone has a leash on that their board won't hit you either. This could easily happen, or the leash could break.

A NOTE FOR BEGINNERS

If you happen to be the out-of-control surfer pay attention! The way I instruct novice students to control their boards is to have them start in a prone position. Once they show me that have some form of control, by steering the board and using the proper weight adjustments, then I teach them how to stand up. In addition, they're taught that wherever they look, is where they'll go. A good way to avoid running someone over is to *see* the surfer or swimmer, in your peripheral vision, but don't *look* at them. If the beginner has their board under control and feels balanced while standing up they're instructed to get low and make a slow turn away from the other person. Further, I teach them to use their upper body as one unit. By getting low in a semi-crouched position, and pointing to where they want to go, their board will follow. If they're not confident doing this (some are and some aren't) then I suggest they go back into a prone position or onto their knees, grab the rails, and steer away from the oncoming person to avoid a collision.

In following these guidelines, use your best judgment.

Remember, there will always be another wave, so please don't risk seriously injuring another surfer for a wave or one more maneuver.

NOTES FOR EVERYONE: DON'T BE A SNAKE

Snaking is any tactic used to impede or steal, a wave from another surfer who's in the priority position. One definition of a snake is someone who paddles around another surfer and takes the wave away from them. Another would be to blatantly drop in on someone. There are many techniques to snaking other surfers, but they're all just different forms of doing the same thing. Trust me, I know every snake move there is and have used all of them at some time or another. Now I only use the knowledge to prevent others from snaking me. Sorry, I'm not going to teach you any more snake moves!

GIVE PEOPLE THEIR SPACE

Another unwritten rule is, if there's someone out surfing alone or even just a few people in the water surfing, look around and see if you can find your own lineup. This could be choosing the next peak over or somewhere further down the beach. In other words, show some respect by not surfing right next to them. Of course, this doesn't apply if there aren't any other waves breaking in the area, or if it's so crowded it doesn't even matter. Yet, even on the crowded days, you can still find some in-between waves to surf. This will give you an opportunity to surf a few alone, although they might not be as good.

19 - THE NEXT WAVE

Although I've shared most of my tricks of the trade to catching more waves with you, there are still a few I've saved up my sleeve. These may be needed for when I *really* get old. With all that's been said, it's quite clear that I'm far from innocent. I'm sure I've snaked as many surfers, guys, and girls, on waves as they have me. Yet, I've probably shared an equal amount of waves for every wave that I've burned someone on.

Come on, everyone I know has been guilty of this infraction at some point or another. Maybe we all have a touch of Miki Dora in us? So, who shall cast the first stone? Not me! Really, it's up to all of us to set a better example by having a positive attitude and maintaining good vibes in and out of the surf for the future generations.

Do yourself a favor, get out there and travel and explore the world.

Keep searching until the day you find your own perfect wave. You may have to get off the beaten path, but that's part of the magic!

For those of you who don't surf, it's hoped that you'll now be educated on the social aspects of surfing, and what the surfers are really doing out in the lineup. If you do decide to start surfing there's still definitely more to learn, but at least now you've been informed of the unwritten, well now written, rules of surfing.

Further, when you get a surfboard and paddle out for your first time, you and everyone else should be safer because of the information that's been shared.

Be creative, and have fun experimenting with some of these methods. Please send me your results and any tricks of your own to catching more waves! I'd like to include some of your stories in one of my future books, for there are still many more tales to tell about the adventures of *Danger Woman*.

"I have searched for, and found, the perfect wave anew. It is called life".
SURF FOR LIFE!
– DW

GLOSSARY OF SURF TERMS

Killer Dana Cartoon 8 1/2 x 11 Ink/Paper

Aerial – When a surfer uses the lip of the wave to launch themselves into the air and then lands back onto the wave to continue their ride. A variety of maneuvers can be performed while in the air.

Aggro - A term for being excessively aggressive.

Airdrop - A late steep drop where your board momentarily leaves the water leaving you suspended in the air before reconnecting with the wave.

Albert "Rabbit" Kekai - *See SURFERS

Aussie - Australian.

Backdoor - Taking off behind the peak and pulling in under the lip of the wave for a tube ride. When you're riding a wave and a section pitches out in front of you allowing you to enter the tube from behind. The name of the right breaking off of the peak at the Banzai Pipeline, Hawaii.

Back peddling - Cross-stepping backward to move back on the board. This is usually done after a nose ride or from the center of the board to get to the tail.

Backside - Surfing with your back to the wave. Example: Goofy footer going right. Regular footer going left.

Bail - Jump off your board. Exit a wave. Leave.

Banked, Banking - Rebounding off of the whitewater to change directions.

Barrel - * See Tube.

Beach Break - Waves that break over sandbars.

Beef of the wave - The best or thickest part of a wave.

Beefy - Powerful or hard-breaking wave. A thick heavy surfboard.

Behind the Curtain - *See Tube

Behind the Peak - Initiating the take-off from behind the pitching part of the wave. This is one way to set up for a tube ride.

Biff it - Wipeout. Make a mistake that ruins your ride or makes you miss a wave.

Bigger Days - When the waves are bigger than the average wave height for that particular surf spot.

Blown out - Wind conditions that break down the open face of the wave (primarily onshore winds but could be from any direction). Least favorable winds for surfing.

Boardless - Being without your surfboard in (or out) of the water. Example: When you lose your board during a wipeout. The waves are good and you don't have your surfboard with you.

Boil - Very shallow area where something is submerged just under the surface of the water making it appear like it's boiling (usually rocks or reefs).

Bomb, Bombing - A huge wave or the biggest wave of the set. To charge or go for it with as much gusto as possible.

Bonehead - *See Yahoo.

Break - When the waves break. A particular surf spot (or location). Type of surf break (point, reef, beach break, etc.). Right or left breaking wave.

Brenda Scott Rodgers - *See SURFERS.

Bro - Short for brother. Friend (Brah - in Hawaiian).

Broken Section - A section of the wave that has fallen (or collapsed), breaking up the previously open face of the wave.

Buckled - When the surfboard has a crease in it from being stressed. Most commonly from hitting the sea floor, rocks or jetty. Once a board is buckled it's common for it to break.

Burn, Burned - To drop in, hop, rip-off or snake another surfer. *See Snake.

Caught Inside - Stuck in front of the breaking waves typically during a set.

Channel - Where the water is deeper between the sand bars, or reefs. Most commonly used to paddle out (or in).

Charge, Charger - A surfer that totally goes for it.

Chick - Girl, woman, female.

Clean, Cleanly - Good surfing conditions or a good ride. Surfing with precision.

Close Out, Closed Out - A section of a wave (or entire wave), that breaks all at once with no shoulder to ride.

Cover up, Covered Up - When the lip of the wave throws over you while you're in the tube.

Cross-stepping - To cross one foot over the other to walk on the board towards the nose (much more stylish than shuffling).

Curl - The area just under the pitching part of the wave forming a hollow section. * See Tube.

Current - *See Ocean Current.

Curtain - The part of the wave once it's throwing out to form a tube obscuring the surfer (behind the curtain). When the tube collapses with the surfer inside (when the curtain closes).

"Da Boyz" - Pidgin (Hawaiian slang) for the boys.

Deck - Top of the surfboard.

Deeper, Deepest - Being the farthest back on the wave for a take-off. Closest to the curl or breaking part of the wave. Way back in the tube.

Delaminate - When the fiberglass (glass) separates from the foam of the surfboard.

Dialed, Dialed-in - Knowing how to do something well. Knowing the details of the lineup or break.

Ding - A crack, shatter, hole or dent on your board that has broken the glass. This can allow water to get in and compromise the integrity of the surfboard.

Double Air Drop - When you have two consecutive airdrops on a wave. *See Air Drop

Down the Line - Riding across the face of the wave, usually to make a section. Something happening further down the wave.

Dropping In - Taking off on a wave. Taking off in front of another surfer *See Snaking.

Dry Haired Session - When you surf a complete session without getting your hair wet. In other words, having no wipeouts or not getting caught inside by the waves.

Dry Reef - When all the water gets sucked off the reef leaving it completely exposed.

Duck Dive - A maneuver used to push you and your board under a wave or the white water when paddling out (mostly done with a short board).

Dude - Man, guy, boy, male, bro.

Duke Paoa Kahinu Mokoe Hulikohola Kahanamoku Aka "The Duke" (1890-1968) - *See SURFERS

Eat It - Wipeout. Fall off of a wave.

Eddie Aikau (1946-1978) - *See SURFERS

Empty - No one out surfing. An unridden wave. No one in the lineup.

Fade - To take-off or bottom turn in the opposite direction that you'll be surfing then turning the other way to ride the wave. This puts you deep on the wave and is one of the several different ways to set up for a tube ride.

Feeding hour - Dusk and dawn when allegedly the sharks like to feed the most. "The only thing predictable about a shark is that they're unpredictable!" (Quote from an Aussie friend).

Flat - When there are no waves breaking or the waves are extremely small.

Floater - Riding along the lip of the wave and dropping back in. Riding up and over the foam to make a section and get back on the open face of a wave.

Foam - *See White Water.

Foam ball - Ball of foam in the pit of the wave or where the white water meets the face of the wave.

Free Surfing Sessions - Anytime you are surfing and not competing.

Frieda Zamba - *See SURFERS.

Gidget (Kathy Kohner) - *See SURFERS.

Ginormous - Extremely giant, beyond huge. Giant, Enormous, and Humongous combined.

Gnarly - Scary, intense or mean.

Goofy-foot - Surfing stance with the right foot forward.

Gringa - Mexican slang for a white girl.

Grom (Gremmie) - A young surfer. There are old groms too. They're the surfers who still get excited to surf anytime, in any surfing conditions, with a youthful outlook. Example: Danger Woman.

Gun, Hawaiian Gun, Rhino Chaser - A Surfboard designed specifically for big hollow waves (usually 9' or longer). A California gun is a toned down version of the Hawaiian Gun.

Haole (HOWL-lay) - Hawaiian term for anyone not from Hawaii (especially a white person).

Hawaiian Beach Boys - Hawaiian surf instructors (starting in the early 1900's). They would take the tourist out surfing and in outrigger canoes.

Hawaiian Style (wave measurement) - The height of the wave based on a Hawaiian wave. In Hawaii, they measure the waves from the back, not the faces. They tend to underestimate the size of the surf (or we overestimate it!).

Head-high - Refers to the height of the wave according to the average height of a male surfer.

Heat - A specified increment of time allotted to catch waves and be scored during a surfing competition

Heaviest - Biggest or most powerful waves. Meanest dude or locals.

Heavy Local Spots - Surf breaks where strangers are unwelcome and the local surfers are aggressive with a territorial attitude.

Heiau (HEY-ow) - Ancient Hawaiian temple or religious sacred site. Puu o Mahuka Heiau - Largest Heiau on Oahu located above Waimea Valley.

High Tide-line - *See Tide-line.

Hog Tied - When your surf leash wraps around you and has you tied up.

Hold Down - When you're held underwater after a wipeout and the wave won't let you up. Sometimes in big surf, you can have a two or three wave hold down.

Hollow - *See Tube.

Hopped, Hopping - *See Snaking.

Howling Offshore - Hard blowing offshore winds that hold the faces of the waves up causing them to pitch, creating hollow waves. *See Winds - Offshore.

Impact Zone - The area where the wave(s) initially crash. This is the hardest breaking part of the wave with the most power. Try to avoid being caught in the impact zone.

In-betweeners - The smaller waves that break between the sets or between lineups.

Inland - Any location not close to the ocean.

Inlander - Anyone who lives inland away from the ocean. My definition would be if you were not within walking or biking distance to the surf.

Inside position - Surfer closest to the breaking part of the wave. The surfer who has the priority position to catch a wave.

Jack-up, Jacked-up - When the wave suddenly lurches up before breaking. This is caused when the wave (or swell) hits a shallow spot. Excited or injured.

Jericho Poplar Bartlow - *See SURFERS.

Jetties - A shoreline structure (consisting of rocks, cement or other materials). Strategically built to redirect, the flow of the water. Intended to help prevent beach erosion. Unfortunately, the long-term effect of some of these structures has caused erosion. They have enhanced waves in some areas and destroyed them in others.

Keiki (KAY-kee) - Hawaiian word for a kid.

Kick out - Exiting the wave. Completing your ride by surfing up and over the back of the wave. Kicking your board out over the back of the wave. There are several different ways to kick out of a wave.

Killer - Really good wave, ride, surf break, surfboard, etc. Dangerous.

Kim Mearig - *See SURFERS.

Knee Boarder - A surfer who rides on, his or her, knees. There are boards made specifically for knee riding called kneeboards.

Kook - Beginner surfer. Someone who's surfed for years, but still surfs (or behaves) like a clueless beginner.

Leash - *See Surf Leash.

Left - A wave that breaks from the right towards the left from a surfer's perspective while paddling into a wave.

Left-hand Break - A wave that breaks from the right towards the left.

Leftovers - The waves that no one else wants or an empty wave that someone has missed or fallen off of. Also, the name of a surf break in Hawaii.

Linda Benson - *See SURFERS.

Lineup - Where the surfers position themselves to catch the waves. Lining up with stationary objects to stay in the best possible position to catch a wave.

Lip - Top part of the wave that is pitching out as the wave is breaking.

Lisa Anderson - *See SURFERS.

Locals - Surfers who live (near), or surf at a particular surf break on a regular basis.

Localism - Locals who aggressively protect their surf break.

Locked-in - When you're in the tube and there's no way out.

Log - Big, thick, heavy longboard.

Longboard - A surfboard that is nine feet or longer, with a wide rounded nose. Official criteria: Longboard must be a minimum length of nine feet measured from nose to tail on the deck of the surfboard. The width dimensions are a total of 47 inches aggregate. This is the total of the widest point, plus the width measured 12 inches up from the tail, and the width measured 12 inches back from the nose.

Lull - The break or resting period between a set of waves.

Lynn Boyer - *See SURFERS.

Mahalo (MAH-Ha-lo) - Hawaiian word for thank you.

Main Break - Where the best most consistent waves are breaking at any given location.

Margo Godfrey Oberg - *See SURFERS.

Mary Lou McGinnis Drummy - *See SURFERS.

Miklos Sandor Dora (1934-2002) - *See SURFERS

Minus or Negative Tide - *See Tide-Line.

Monster - A giant, huge, humungous or ginormous wave.

Mush-ball, Mushy - Slow breaking or rolling wave with very little power or push.

Nose - The front tip of the surfboard.

Nose-dive - *See Pearl.

Nose-ride - Surfing with one foot (hang five) or both feet (hang ten) on the nose (tip) of the surfboard.

Ocean Current - An underwater river flowing in one direction. They can be close to shore or in the deep oceans. Also, can be temporary or for long durations.

Offshore - *See Winds.

Off-the-Lip - A vertical turn off of the top pitching part (lip) of the wave.

Open Face - The rideable part of the wave that is not foam or whitewater.

Outside - When the waves are approaching from outside of the lineup. Waves that break the furthest out.

Over-the-falls - A wipeout where you get thrown over with the pitching part (lip) of the wave.

Packed - Very crowded.

Paddle - To use your arms in a swim-like motion for forward momentum to propel your surfboard.

Paddle Battle - Surfers trying to out paddle or maneuver each other to catch a wave. This includes racing back out to the lineup.

Paddle out - Paddling your surfboard out through the surf to the lineup. The ceremony for the passing of a surfer. Surf communities tradition of a funeral service.

Peak - The crest of the wave. The highest part of the wave before the wave breaks.

Pearl, Pearling, Nose-dive - When the nose of the surfboard penetrates the water and catapults the surfer in front of the board and the wave. This is most common on the take-off but can happen after any maneuver when coming off the top back down the face of the wave. I believe they call it pearling because it sends you to the bottom where you can dive for pearls.

Peter "P.T." Townend - *See SURFERS.

Pick off - To select a wave.

Pit, Pitted - Deepest part of the wave. Deep-in-the-tube. *See Tube.

Pitched, Pitching - When the top part (lip) of the wave tosses the surfer. The lip or top part of the wave is throwing out.

Point Break - Waves that break predominantly in one direction off of a promontory or point of land into a bay. Could be a rock, reef or sand point which can be visible (exposed) or submerged.

Racks, Surf Racks - Racks specifically designed to go on the top of a car to secure and transport surfboards (also made for bicycles and customized for motorcycles).

Rails - Side edges of the surfboard.

Rail Saver - A flat piece of nylon material at the end of the surf leash that attaches to the string. This was designed to prevent the urethane cord from cutting through the rail of the surfboard.

Rashguard, Rashie - An under shirt made of Spandex and Nylon originally used to prevent from getting rashes or to protect you from the Sun when surfing without a wetsuit. However, if it got windy it would make you really cold. They were also worn under a wetsuit for more warmth. With modern technology there is now a rashguard that's made with a special material (Koredry). This material has UV protection and repels the water to keep you from getting cold when the winds start blowing.

Reef - Rock or Coral formations.

Reef Break - Waves that break over coral or rock reefs (can be exposed, or submerged, or a combination thereof).

Re-entry - To surf out the back or over the top of the wave, re-entering into the wave.

Regular-foot, Natural foot - Surfing stance with the left foot placed forward.

Rell Sunn - *See SURFERS.

Right or Left - Direction the waves are breaking. Direction the surfer is riding a wave. This is always done from the surfer's perspective while looking towards the shore from the water.

Rip, Ripping, Ripping it up - Surfing really good. *Also See Riptide or Rip Current.

Rip Current – A strong current of water flowing seaward or along the shoreline.

Riptide - A strong current of water flowing seaward due to a tidal change.

Rock Dance - The act of having to walk over rocks (submerged or exposed), to get out to the waves or back in towards shore. Some rock dances can be very dangerous with sharp lava rocks or coral, rebar, broken glass, sea urchins or other sea life.

Roundhouse Cutback - Turning back towards the breaking part of the wave and banking off of the foam to redirect the board back down the line. This is really two connected turns forming a figure eight.

Sandbar - Built up mound (or bar) of sand created by the rips or currents pushing the sand to the side. Also, by stationary objects breaking the flow of the water like large rocks, piers, jetties, etc.

Scratch, Scratching - Refers to paddling hard to get over the waves or to prevent getting caught inside by a set. Paddling hard into a wave to catch it. Paddling fast out to the lineup for wave priority.

Secret Spot - A surf spot that only a few surfers know about. A hidden surf break.

Session - The time period in which you are out surfing. It's not uncommon to have a couple of surf sessions (or more) in a single day.

Set - A series of waves that comes in intervals.

Set Wave - Any one of the waves in a set. Many times refers to the biggest wave of the set.

Seven-six - Refers to the length of a surfboard in reference to feet and inches. Seven feet six inches (7'6").

Shacked - When a surfer gets totally tubed. Getting a really deep barrel.

Shape - The form of the wave. The outline of the surfboard.

Shapely - Good shaped waves.

Sharky - Shark filled waters. Surf breaks that are notorious for sharks frequenting.

Shore-break - The waves that break on the shore.

Shoulder - The part of the wave that tapers off or slopes off away from the peak.

Shoulder Hopping - Taking off on the shoulder of the wave in front of another surfer who's already riding the wave (or taking off deeper). *See Snake.

Shut down - When the top of the wave collapses or closes out. When the waves suddenly go flat.

Shred, Shredding - Surfing really radical. * See Ripping.

Sick - Really good. Could be a wave, ride, day, etc. Example: "What a sick ride!"

Side-shore Current - When you have a strong current of water pulling parallel to the beach as opposed to pulling out. Another form of rip current. The water movement up, or down, the beach due to the swell direction.

Sit - Sitting on your surfboard. Waiting for a wave (in the lineup). Used to get a better view of the approaching waves (set) or to spin it around to catch a wave. Or to spin it seaward to paddle back out when you miss a wave.

Sketched, Sketched Out - Scared.

Smaller Days - When the waves are smaller than usual at any given break.

Snake, Snaking - Burning, Cutting-off, Dropping in On, Hopping, Shoulder Hopping, Etc. - Any form of taking (stealing) a wave from another surfer. Examples: Dropping in front of another surfer who's already riding a wave. Paddling around someone who's in the priority position. Spinning around and taking off underneath someone, Etc.

Soup - *See White Water.

Spaghetti Arms - When your arms are so tired from paddling you can barely take another stroke.

Speed Wobbles - When you get going too fast on a skateboard and it starts wiggling out of control. Usually just before you fall.

Spit - When the compressed air in the tube gets blown out. When a surfer gets blown out of the tube.

Split, Split the Peak - To leave. Two surfers sharing a wave by surfing in opposite directions.

Spot - Surf spot, surf break, surfing location.

Stall - Slowing the board down to stay in the curl or more critical part of the wave.

Stick - Surfboard.

Stoked - Exceedingly Happy.

Straight-off-Adolph - When someone (usually a beginner) drops in going straight towards the beach instead of traversing across the wave.

Stuffed - When one surfer forces another surfer so far back into the wave (or whitewater) that they can't make the wave. This can be done on the take-off too.

Suck-out Section - When the wave sucks out due to a very shallow section.

SUP - Stand Up Paddleboard - A surfboard designed to be ridden while continuously standing and using a paddle to propel it, catch waves, and turn.

Surfable - A rideable wave. Good (or good enough) surf conditions.

Surf Animal - A die-hard surfer who can never get enough waves. An aggressive surfer who charges (especially in big surf).

Surf Crazed - Totally obsessed with surfing.

Surfing Etiquette - The established code of behavior in a surfing society or amongst a group of surfers.

Surf Leash, Leash, Cord, Goon Cord, Leg Rope, Leggy, etc. - A flexible urethane cord designed to attach the surfboard to the surfer so the board stays with them.

Surf Stomp - A party of surfers. Usually with loud music, a Hawaiian theme and plenty of beer and making out. Surfers dancing at a surf party.

Swell - Swells are moving masses of water created by winds. The longer and harder the winds blow, the bigger the swell. This energy can travel thousands of miles before hitting something shallow (primarily a sandbar, point, reef, rock), forming it into a breaking wave. The more drastic the change from deep water to shallow water, the bigger and more powerful the wave.

Swing Wide, Swinger - A wave that breaks wide or further over from where the majority of the waves are breaking. Most common at a point break.

Take-off - The beginning part of the ride when you first drop into a wave.

Tandem Surfing - When two riders ride on the same board while surfing. Typically, the man will lift the woman while she performs a series of gymnastic-like moves. There are surfboards designed specifically for tandem surfing and tandem surfing competitions. Surfing Pregnant.

Tearing it up - Performing really radical maneuvers.

Tide - The influx and receding flow of water caused by the gravitational pull of the sun and the moon.

Tide Line - 0.0, Low, High, Minus (negative).

- 0.0 Tide - This is the invisible tide line determined by scientist approximately every 20 years by calculating the gravitational pull of the sun and the moon.
- High Tide - The highest tides during any 24-hour period.
- High Tide Line - The highest point of where the water has come up the beach. Usually visible where the wet sand meets the dry sand. There are private beaches where the laws allow access only if you stay below the high tide line.
- Low Tide - The lowest tides during any 24-hour period.
- Minus (negative) Tide - When the tide is below the 0.0 tide line.

Tomb-stoning - When the nose of a surfboard is sticking up out of the water like a grave marker. This is due to someone being held down or dragged underneath the surface of the water (only if wearing a leash). If you see this happening pay close attention in the event they may need immediate rescuing. This is common in big surf.

Tube - Barrel, Behind the Curtain, Cover-up, Curl, Pit, Greenroom, Hollow, Shack, Tunnel, Etc. - The inside part of the wave that is covered by the lip throwing over, creating a hollow tunnel.

Tube-ride - Surfing in the hollow tunnel of the wave behind the curtain. This is the ultimate reward of surfing and is truly one of the top most exhilarating feelings in the world. Due to its difficulty, and the skill required to get in (and out), of the tube, it's the highest scoring maneuver in competitive surfing.

Tubular - Hollow conditions.

Tunnel - *See Tube.

Turtle Turn - A method used to get a board (most commonly a longboard), under a wave when paddling out. This is done by flipping the board upside down while going under the wave (or foam).

Wahine (WA-hee-neh) - Hawaiian word for girl or woman.

Walled, Walled up - *See Close Out.

Wave Chasing - Driving up and down the coast checking numerous surf spots for the best surf. Chasing unpredictable peaks up and down the beach trying to catch a wave. Following the swells for the biggest waves. Example: Big wave surfers will surf the same swell within a few days starting in Hawaii (Waimea, Oahu or Jaws in Maui), following it to Northern California (Mavericks), then down to Mexico (Todos Santos Island off of Ensenada in Baja California).

Wave Fest - Catching an abundance of waves.

Wave Hog - Someone who takes (hogs), all the waves and doesn't take turns or share with others.

Wave Hunt - *See Wave Chasing.

Weekend Warrior - Surfer who predominantly surfs only on the weekends.

Wetsuit - A full (or partial) body suit made of neoprene (or rubber), designed to keep surfers warm in cold water or prevent them from being scraped on rocks or reefs.

Whitewash - *See White Water.

White Water, Whitewash, Foam, Soup - The foamy broken part of the wave that has already crashed (or been blown) down.

Winds -
- Glassy - Calm or no winds.
- Offshore - blowing off the land seaward.
- Onshore - blowing off the sea towards the land.
- Side shore - blowing sideways across the waves.

Wipe Out - To fall or get knocked off of your board.

Worked - Slammed, beat up or tossed around by the waves. Bad wipe out. Being held under by the surf for a long time.

Yahoo - A clueless inexperienced surfer. A Kook bully with a bad attitude. Anyone one with stupid behavior while surfing (including experienced surfers).

SURF BREAKS

Arthurs Beach 8 x 10 Acrylic/Canvas

CALIFORNIA

Blackies (Newport Pier) - Newport Beach, North Orange County
Named after the local bar in the adjacent parking lot.

Cardiff - San Diego County.

Huntington Beach - North Orange County
   - Surf City, U.S.A.

Malibu (Surfrider Beach) - Los Angeles County

MY GRANDMA SURFS BETTER THAN YOU

The Ranch - Santa Barbara County
- Bixby Ranch - Private Beach
- Hollister Ranch - Private Beach

Rincon - Santa Barbara County
- Indicators - the furthest point out at Rincon
- River mouth
- Cove

San Onofre - South Orange County/North San Diego County border
- The Point
- Four Doors
- Old Man's
- Dog Patch
- Trails (one through six).

T-Street (Trafalgar Street) - San Clemente, Orange County
Located just south of the San Clemente Pier.

Trestles - San Clemente, Orange County
- Cottons Point (northern most point at Trestles).
- Barbwires (between Uppers and Cottons).
- Uppers (Upper trestles).
- 5 O's (Between Uppers and Lowers - rarely breaks here).
- Lowers (Lower Trestles).
- Middles (between Lowers and Churches).
- Churches (the last point before San Onofre to the South).

HAWAII

North Shore, Oahu
- Backdoor - the right breaking off of the peak at Pipeline.
- Haleiwa

- Lani's (Laniakea)
- Pipeline (Banzai Pipeline).
- Rocky Point
- Sunset Beach
- Turtle Bay - (towards East Side).
- Velzyland
- Waimea Bay (The Bay).

South Shore, Oahu
- Waikiki

West Side, Oahu
- Makaha

Costa Rican Glow 9 X 12 Oil/Canvas

MEXICO

Cantamar - Baja California
A trailer park south of Rosarita Beach.

Puerto Escondido aka "The Mexican Pipeline" - Oaxaca.
Located in the southern part of Mainland Mexico.
Known to be one of the most dangerous surfing waves in the world.

OREGON

The Cove - Can't Say Where, Or What County
Also, a surf spot in Palos Verde, CA - Some places around the world
have the same name for a surf break.

SURFERS

Gidget and Kim - Malibu 2015   Photo: Duncan McKenzie

*Albert "Rabbit" Kekai aka *"Uncle Rabbit"* (1920 - 2016) - One of the innovators of modern hot-dog surfing (radical surfing maneuvers). Hawaiian Beach Boy (tutored by the Duke). 4-time U.S.A. Surfing Champion 1973, 1980, 1984, 1988. Inducted into the Surfing Walk of Fame 2001. Inducted into the Surfing Hall of Fame 2012.

Brenda Scott Rodgers - 1978 World Cup Surfing Champion. Santa Cruz pro surfer and big wave charger. Brenda was one of the first professional women surfers. Daughter of 'Doc' Scott (Doc's Pro Plugs). The Owner of Hotline Wetsuits, president of International Aquatic Trades, Inc. Nominee Surfing Walk of Fame 2016.

*Dr. Bruce Gabrielson, Ph.D. aka "Snake" - Bruce is not only an accomplished and successful contest surfer, he organized many championship surfing events, mentored and coached many outstanding competitive surfers, shaped boards for his company Wave Trek, and has served in surfing leadership positions since the 1960s. He founded the Edison HS surf club, organized the first high school surfing league and was the first varsity surf coach at Huntington Beach High School. He is currently founder and chairman of the National Surf Schools and Instructors Association.

David Nuuiwha - First off, David is one of the best all-time nose riders ever! U.S.A. National Champion in 1968 and 1971. Inducted into the Surfing Walk of Fame 2001 under the Local Hero category and again in 2005 as a Surfing Champion. Inducted into the Surfing Hall of Fame in 2004 in Huntington Beach. Appeared in numerous surf flicks as well as Jimi Hendrix's movie 'Rainbow Bridge'.

*Duke Kahanamoku (1890 - 1968) aka "Father of Modern Surfing" or simply "The Duke" - The Duke introduced surfing to the world during his travels as an Olympic athlete. He's a five-time Olympic Medalist (3 gold, 2 silver), between 1912 and 1924. Inducted into the Surfing Walk of Fame in 1994. Inducted into International Swimming Hall of Fame 1965. Inducted into U.S. Olympic Hall of Fame 1984. The Sheriff of Honolulu, Hawaii from 1934 to1961. I believe most would agree that "The Duke" is the most revered surfer of our times.

Edward "Eddie" Aikau (1946 - 1978) - First place at the prestigious Duke Kahanamoku Invitational Surf Contest 1977. Inducted into the Surfing Walk of Fame 2000. The first Eddie Aikau Memorial Surf Contest was 1986 in which his beloved brother Clyde won. Eddie was one of the very best big wave riders, and the first professional lifeguard at Waimea Bay on the North Shore of Oahu, Hawaii. Eddie is a very highly respected waterman.

Frieda Zamba - World Surfing Champion 1984, 1985, 1986, 1988 Inducted into the Surfing Walk of Fame 1998.

Jericho Poplar Bartlow - World Surfing Champion 1976. Second in the World in 1979. Co-founder of Women's International Surfing Association (WISA). Co-founder of the Golden Girls. A major promoter of women's surfing. Founded Kids for Clean Water. Environmental activist. Inducted into the Surfing Walk of Fame in 1997. Inducted into the Surfing Hall of Fame in 2004.

Jimmy Hogan - Pro surfer from the 80's and early 90's. Currently, runs his own surf camp in Costa Rica.

*Joyce Hoffman - World Surfing Champion 1965, 1966. Inducted into the Surfing Walk of Fame 1994. Joyce dominated Women's Surfing in the 60's.

Kathy "Gidget" Kohner Zuckerman - Kathy Kohner the original "Gidget". A Book: "Gidget, The Little Girl with Big Ideas" released in 1957 (later a movie and then a TV series) that helped to over-popularize surfing in the late 50's and early 60's.

Kim Mearig - World Surfing Champion 1983, Inducted into the Surfing Walk of Fame 2002.

Linda Benson - First woman to surf Waimea. U.S.A. Surfing Champion 1959, 1960, 1961, 1964 and 1968. Inducted into the Surfing Walk of Fame in 1997.

Lisa Anderson - World Surfing Champion 1994, 1995, 1996, 1997. Inducted into the Surfing Walk of Fame in 2004. Inducted into the Surfing Hall of Fame in 2002.

Lynn Boyer - World Surfing Champion in 1978 and 1979. Inducted into the Surfing Walk of Fame in 2008, and the Hawaii Sports Hall of Fame in 2009. Lynn is also a very accomplished artist.

Margo Godfrey Oberg - One of the first professional women surfers. World Surfing Champion 1968, 1976, 1977, 1980 and 1981. Inducted into the Surfing Walk of Fame in 1995. Inducted into the Surfing Hall of Fame in 1991. A pioneer for professional women surfers. Big wave charger.

*Mary Lou McGinnis Drummy - Surfing competitor in the 50's, 60's and 70's. Co-founder of W.I.S.A. (Women's International Surfing Association). Ran the Wahine series in the 90's. A major promoter for amateur surfing - U.S.S.F. (United States Surfing Federation). Now called W.S.A. (World Surfing Association) of which she is currently the executive director. Midget Smith Judging Award 2014. Inducted into the Surfing Walk of Fame 2016.

Miklos Sandor Dora (1934 - 2002) - aka "Da Cat", "Black Knight of Surfing", "Malibu Miki" (to name a few) - The ultimate surf rebel who would do anything (and to anyone), to his advantage to get more waves or advance his position in life. Miki was a surf purist that set an example of how to be a perpetual surfer for life. As the saying goes, "Dora Lives!"

Peter "P.T." Townend - World Surfing Champion 1976. Co-founder of the Bronzed Aussies. Inducted into the Surfing Walk of Fame 1998. Australian Surfing Hall of Fame 2001. Inducted into the Surfing Hall of Fame 2004. He is one of the major players in turning surfing into a professional sport. P.T. is an icon in the professional world of surfing.

Rell Sunn (1950 - 1998) aka "The Queen of Makaha", "Auntie Rell" - World Class Surfer. Inducted into the Surfing Walk of Fame in 1996. The first woman to lifeguard in Hawaii (1975). Known for her smooth style and Aloha attitude. Rell was one of the most revered female surfers. Overall, excellent water-women.

All of these surfers I've mention have many more accomplishments than listed. This information barely does them justice. Each and every one of them has excelled in surfing, *The Sport of Kings and Queens*. I suggest researching surfing history for inspiration from the men and women who have helped pave the way for what modern surfing is today, for I've only mention a few.

* Not mentioned in the book but worthy of mention for their contribution to the surfing community.

ABOUT THE AUTHOR

By

Dr. Bruce Gabrielson, Ph.D

aka *"Snake"*

Kim Hamrock, widely known in the surf world as *Danger Woman*, caught her first wave at thirteen years old. It wasn't until the age of sixteen when she started surfing seriously. Her competitive career didn't begin until she was a month shy of her thirtieth birthday. At this point, she was married with a family of three kids. Known for pushing the limits in the big wave arena, she raised the bar for the next generation of women surfers. With twelve U.S.A. championship titles, six West Coast championships, one East Coast championship, and numerous other titles under her belt. Kim is truly a force to be reckoned with. At age 42 she became the 2002 Women's World Longboard Surfing Champion, and in 2005 was inducted into the prestigious Surfing Walk of Fame. In June 2015, Kim participated in setting 2 Guinness World Records in one day; "Most people riding one surfboard" (total 66) on the "Largest surfboard" ever created, measuring a staggering 42'.

Kim has been interviewed on television and radio internationally, as well as being featured in major publications such as *Sports Illustrated Magazine* (August 16, 1993). Also, Kim is a contributing writer for surfing instructional books. Furthermore, she has produced her own surfing instructional DVD, *Safe Surfing with Danger Woman*. In addition, she wrote the Water Wisdom column for *Wahine Magazine* (the first all women's surfing magazine), and helped Carlos Davis (writer of Drop Dead Fred), with the rewrites for a full feature surfing comedy.

Although now retired as a professional competitor, Kim continues to instruct and travel, sharing her passion for surfing with thousands of people throughout the world. She is a Master Surf Instructor and one of the founders of the National Surf School and Instructors Association (NSSIA). Lastly, has operated her own surf school since 1995.

When not surfing, she spends her time working as an artist, musician, and author. This book documents her many adventures and modus operandi. Kim's lifestyle continues to influence and inspire women surfers, reaching for their own dreams.

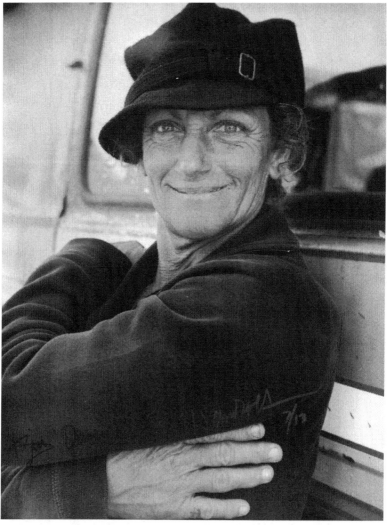

Kim Hamrock   Photo: Bill Hopkins

Kim Hamrock- Surfing Walk of Fame Women of the year 2005

Kim with her Pipeline trophies and friend Vivian

CONTACT INFORMATION

Kim Hamrock
P.O. Box 183
Huntington Beach, CA 92648

E-mail: Kim@dangerwoman.com
Dangerwoman007@gmail.com

Website: www.DangerWoman.com

Facebook: https://www.facebook.com/kimhamrock

Instagram: https://www.instagram.com/dangerwoman.art

Twitter: https://twitter.comDangerWomanArt

Blog: https://dangerwomanbook.blogspot.com

Go Fund Me:
https://funds.gofundme.com/dashboard/dangerwoman

Book Orders: https://www.amazon.com/dp/1541222105

https://www.createspace.com/5406863

Contact Artist/Cartoonist: Kim Hamrock

Made in the USA
San Bernardino, CA
30 October 2017